D/2023/45/51 – ISBN 978 94 014 9028 3 – NUR 800

Cover design: Atelier Steve Reynders
Interior design: Gert Degrande | De Witlofcompagnie
Illustrations avatars: Annemie Berebrouckx

LannooCampus Publishers is a subsidiary of Lannoo Publishers,
the book and multimedia division of Lannoo Publishers nv.

LannooCampus Publishers
Vaartkom 41 Box 01.02   P.O. Box 23202
3000 Leuven   1100 DS Amsterdam
Belgium   Netherlands
www.lannoocampus.com

Ihsane Haouach

OPEN UP YOUR ORGANI- SATION

Fully Embrace Diversity with Profiles Inclusiveness

Lannoo
Campus

OPENNESS   PATIENCE

NATURAL   EMPATHY

Table of contents

**OPEN
UP
YOUR
ORGANI-
SATION**

Introduction

No does not mean no

I grew up in a family where debates are normal. When I wanted to do something new, my father generally answered "No". It's not that he did not listen or pay attention to my desires. On the contrary, my dad was present and attentive, much more than men of his generation. It's just that if in doubt, refusing is safer than accepting. My father is a man of prudence; he rarely pronounces words to be regretted. My mother is the opposite; she is a woman of action. If she is wrong, that's not a problem – she will never admit it. She has a way of changing the subject with such audacity that few can challenge. She insisted that we ask her permission before asking my father. She said: "I need to prepare him. You know your father. I will deal with him." That was not the only reason: she wanted to feel that she had more influence, and she knew that information is power. Whenever I turned to my mum to ask for something new, she stared at me with her suspicious look and started questioning me. In another life, she could have been a cop: you are guilty until proven otherwise. If you asked to hang out with a friend, she suspected the presence of another fellow, who was a less suitable date.

Generally, she was right. Her sixth sense is lie detection. In my case, it's omission detection. As a matter of principle, I have always hated lying, but I'm also terrible at it. So my strategy was to reveal as few things as possible: technically, if you don't give a piece of information, you are not lying – you "forgot". For this tactic to work, you cannot be asked the question, and you could rarely avoid my mother's cross-examination. Only if I was able to convince her, could I go to my father. Of course, he could not know that I had spoken to her before. He was the head of the family, he was the one making the decision; at least, it had to appear this way. My mother had to look as if she had heard the story for the first time. As she was also not a good liar (proof that it does not take one to know one), she often occupied herself during the conversation. My father took his time to give the two-letter answer. He listened, waited a few seconds while he looked me in the eyes and I stared at the floor (watch out for the cultural trap: in Arab culture, you don't look into the eyes of a person in authority), then, my hope for an easy three-letter answer was ravaged by… "No". The next words I uttered were of consequence: they determined whether a discussion would follow or not. If my nerves were not contained, for instance if my tone rose, the "no" would become definitive. Surprisingly, in most cases, the "no" flipped into a "we will see", increasing the probability of a "yes". It is like when it's raining and suddenly there is a ray of light. "Catch the sun before it's gone," sang Doves[1].

My parents taught me that **openness** to other viewpoints is natural, and these three basic lessons have been ingrained in me:
1. Getting something requires that it is deserved
2. Never take no for an answer.
3. Words are powerful.

With us, against them

When I was sent to Hungary to develop a cutting-edge business control system, the assignment seemed daunting: framing and implementing a project with the ambition to use the same tool across all European subsidiaries. The roll-out in Brussels had already been a difficult experience. Before leaving, I received a full briefing on the technical and business aspects. Although useful, it was not the most helpful. Three legal entities coexisted: each one had its own culture. The number of expatriates from France and Belgium was proportionally too high. Stereotypes were well entrenched in labour relations: French culture was perceived as too imposing; the Belgian way, more pragmatic except when community conflicts were imported. This separated one visible group into three: Flanders, Wallonia, and Brussels. The project was due in six months: the deadline was tight. The first four weeks were a complete waste of time. The straightforward nature of my management style hit three walls until I realised that I had completely ignored the human factor. I needed a period to get to know them, show an interest in their culture, gain their trust, and move out of the professional framework. Caring about your colleagues is not only a positive act but also an investment.

Change management requires **patience**. You can start slowly and then accelerate to catch up on the plan only if there is trust and agreement on a common goal. I did not take the time to step back and ask valuable questions. Why should they accept a management tool enabling someone from afar to control their finances, and therefore make decisions while not understanding their business as well as they do? Of course they did not want it. They were doing everything in their power to block any advancements and stop me if I was interfering.

I made many mistakes. The first one was to assume that because top management makes decisions, people follow orders. I had to convince them that the project would benefit them with or without the head office. The second one was to consider them as one group. Three companies were merging, and none of them wanted the others. How could they embrace a common tool if they did not mean to be together? I needed to show them the advantages of merging. The third one was to stick to deadlines set by headquarters: milestones should be discussed and agreed on with the local teams. The fourth one was to try to be too quick. I had to be much more patient, to work for long-term results rather than checking some boxes. At the end of the project, I was asked to stay in Budapest. "You are with us and know how to talk to them," the locals said. "You know how to work with them while being one of us," the headquarters complimented me. In their minds, there was an "us" versus "them". There always is…

Hearing is not feeling

Openness and patience are needed in order to understand people and put yourself in their shoes. It was when I wrote and performed in a theatre play that I realised how necessary empathy was.

During my studies at Solvay Business School, I had long hours of discussions with some students who couldn't understand some of my personal choices. I am talking about people of good faith who respect you for whatever decision you make for yourself. They were just not familiar with the diversity of origins. I specifically mention their sincere intentions because, for me, it makes all the difference. It is not about convincing, but about understanding, which makes the exchange more valuable for everyone involved. For a dialogue to be true, you need to feel entitled to be yourself. Whenever you feel you are being judged, you will think twice before talking, you will hide some facts, you will speak cautiously, or even stop the conversation prematurely. Those comrades came to my theatre play[2], where this specific subject was addressed. The scene lasted four and a half minutes. In those 275 seconds, spectators laughed and cried, sometimes simultaneously. This was enough to make my friends understand me, better than hours of debates. One came to me, disoriented, and said:

- Ihsane, I understand now. I'm sorry. I did not realise.
- Thank you, it means a lot. But why are you sorry?
- Because we hurt you. Society hurts you. And I'm sorry on behalf of all of us. I did not know.
- But I told you...
- Yes, I heard you, but I did not understand it. Now I do.

Later, another acquaintance revealed that he had shed a tear. This is **empathy**. With a theatre play, the public listens, sees, and mostly feels your emotions. My comic skills aren't great; nevertheless, I was able to perform that scene very well because I felt every word and every action of Mounia, my heroine. She was pure fiction, but she was me, my sister-in-law, my friend, my student, and, thanks to empathy, every person in that room (now, don't ask me why I named her Mounia, I have no clue...).

Self-pressure to not be

Once I entered professional life, I felt that I needed to work harder and couldn't fail. I perceived a lot of pressure to deliver perfect, excellent work. When completing my first evaluation, I asked what caused the missing 0.5: 4.5 on 5 implies something was not well done, what was it? My managers explained that it was impossible to obtain 5, that 4.5 was the maximum they could give, and that I should be happy. I was not. This lacking 0.5 frightened me. I was under such stress that when team building was organised during Ramadan, I did not speak up. I knew that having a full day of sports activities in the summer was going to be hard. I was in good physical condition; at that time, I was jogging and going to the gym twice or three times a week (unfortunately, that is not the case any more...). For the entire day, I participated more than my colleagues. I had to prove that fasting had no impact on my work performance, even in cohesion activities. I had to show that having a Muslim on the team was not a handicap. I remember walking on a wire several metres above sea level, climbing a wall without hooks, running like crazy... My colleague, Stephane, and I were the two best performers. During the afternoon, I felt dizzy. I went to the restroom and locked myself in there for fifteen minutes. You might think it's normal: intense cardio sport without water or sugar for hours. When I went out, Stephane asked me if all was well: "How are you feeling? If you need to rest, no worries, I can replace you for an exercise." "No thank you," I answered. He insisted, "Nobody will blame you; you are fast..." Without letting him finish his sentence, I called my colleagues, who were on a break: "Come on, you lazy guys! We need to continue!" The day closed with a barbecue. My director, Gwen, noticed that I was not eating, and asked me why. I said that I was fasting. She was sorry. She blamed herself for not knowing; she blamed me for not speaking up. "The team building could have been scheduled next week; it would not have been an issue." Then she asked her assistant to consider Ramadan on the list of events for next year. She prepared my dish and asked the trainer to keep it warm for me. Gwen was embarrassed. She knew me. She understood the efforts I made to be "normal". What if, instead of being normal, I was **natural**?

After that experience, I realised that it is in the common interest for everyone to be themselves. In my denial of difference, I pushed myself in a physically dangerous way, I embarrassed Gwen (who later became my mentor) and I did not reach the goal of the day, which was to have fun in an integrated team. Today, I admit without shame that it feels so empowering to be just... natural!

Difference is the new normal

One morning I was styling the hair of my daughter, and I asked her whether she wanted a high or low chignon. She answered "normal". I understood what she meant. Then I asked myself: "What is normal?" How can a four-year-old child have a conception of what is *normal* or what is not? A simple rule of thumb is to consider what is seen most often as *normal*. We are used to seeing a board of directors of white men above fifty years old. It's *normal* but not necessarily good, or bad. It will be determined by their actions, which are derived from their thoughts, which arise from their experiences, which are shaped by their personalities and their biases. It is possible to have a room full of white men who are extremely diverse, as well as a room with men and women of different skin tones sharing a similar opinion. The nomination of Joe Biden is a suitable example. One can say: "Once again, an old white man in the White House", or "The first Ivy League-degree-free president in 36 years".

Of course, any selection criteria should be examined: was there any direct or indirect discrimination? Do the candidates represent the diversity within society in all its aspects, visible and not? More broadly: are education, employment, and housing access in the society equal, as this will generally determine the chance of success? Observing a person's physical characteristics alone is useful but not enough. Beyond appearances, each of us has a personality and a bias formed by our socio-economic and cultural background, our education, our community, our religious and non-religious beliefs, our generation, our ambitions … Our sensory organs and filters operate without us even realising it. One should accept that there is no absolute reality. Reality is subjective. Truth is subjective. Most of us are familiar with the famous image of one person showing a nine and the other showing a six. Both argue that the other is wrong. Essentially, they are both right, but wrong in disputing the other's point of view. How can they be right if the reality is different? Because it's *their* reality, not *the* reality.

" Nobody,

Nobody can be sure they're always right.

The ones who are fullest of themselves that way

Are the emptiest vessels. "

Seamus Heaney³

Dear reader,

Through this introduction, you see where I am heading. This book presents the OPEN way, a novel perspective based on the profile inclusiveness. The concept of diversity, equity, inclusion, and inclusiveness goes beyond appearances. It encompasses everything that makes us unique among the eight billion people living on this planet. The "OPEN way" I modelled is not drastically different, yet disruptive.

Before going further, I would like to make a pact with you. If you are holding this book in your hand, it means that you are ready to embark on a journey with me. Let's make the most of it. Please be:

- **Open to my viewpoint**: My thoughts are based on my personal and professional experiences, my personality, and my vision. They can evolve, they can remain. It is perfectly fine to agree and disagree with some of my statements, to like or dislike some principles and, certainly, I encourage you to question everything you read. Disagreeing does not make us enemies; agreeing does not make us friends.

" *Look at situations from all angles, and you will become more open.* **"** **Dalai Lama**

- **Patient with my explanations**: Openness needs patience. I might tell you a lot of stories, but all of it has a purpose. Do not close the book until you have read the last word. It may take time for an idea to fully sink in. Reading takes time. Yet, what do we have left if we don't devote the necessary time to learning?

> **"** *Patience is bitter, but its fruit is sweet.* **"**

Jean-Jacques Rousseau

- **Empathic with the anecdotes:** Put yourself in another person's shoes, whether it is mine or one of my interviewees. Let your emotions guide you through the stories, and feel free to absorb another person's experiences. Your mind can only be opened to other possibilities when you release control.

> **"** *I think we all have empathy. We may not have enough courage to display it.* **"**
Maya Angelou

- **(Be) Natural**: Find the space in which you are yourself. The more aware you are of yourself, the more likely you are to listen to other perspectives. To trust others, you need to trust yourself. To listen to others, you need to listen to yourself. You are not me or any of the people I have interviewed. You may recognise yourself or someone you know in the stories, you may not. It's okay, as long as you're open, patient, empathic, and natural, you will not miss the point.

> **"** *To be yourself in a world that is constantly trying to make you something else is the greatest accomplishment.* **"**
Ralph Waldo Emerson

Presentations

Diversity and inclusion are topics that people often discuss with me. Until last year, my answer was the same:

"I am not here to talk about diversity. I'm tired of discussing it. Why are you putting me in that box? My expertise is in change management and knowledge transmission.

Of course, I talk about diversity, of course, it is important for any project, specifically for change. But not in the way it is discussed in the mainstream today. Diversity in society is not the same as diversity in a company. So, treating it the same way does not make sense."

That's how the adventure of this book started. I was discussing my career with Thierry Geerts, CEO of Google Belgium. He thought that my views on diversity should be shared, and even more so when I explained why I don't want to talk about them. Francis Blake, chairman of Derbigum, was very supportive of this idea: "It makes complete sense! You are *the* person who should write about diversity!"

I was intrigued by their advice, yet I was already busy with another writing project, so I parked the suggestion somewhere below my left brain. After closing it, the idea popped up, as if it was waiting for the button "free space" in my mind. Does my view deserve a book? Is it unique? Who am I to write a management book? I shared my questions with Thibaut Georgin, who presented me to Alexandre Pycke, who introduced me to Isabel Verstraete, writer of the CARE principles. After a wonderful evening sharing our stories, I decided that the idea was worth investigating. Isabel was so enthusiastic that she even introduced me to my current editor, LannooCampus.

I was still not convinced. All my life, I've done things because *I have to*. I am in a phase where I only answer to *I want to*. My mind created the model OPEN during a non-productive afternoon, completely unannounced. I wanted to verify the market value of the concept before going forward. Therefore, I shared this ambitious plan with other leaders, such as Ilham Kadri, Pierre Gurdjian, Audrey Hanard, Hanan Challouki, Mikaël Wornoo and Ibrahim Ouassari.

"Wonderful idea."

"Of course, you should."

"You are the one to talk about it! You have so much experience to share!"

"Can I write a preface?"

Then, I asked them, "Would you like to contribute?"
Unanimously, the answer was yes. They all trusted me with their stories, and for that I am extremely grateful.

The twelve individuals in this book were not selected at random. Initially, I considered their character, their experiences, and the environment in which they evolved. After completing my list, I performed a basic calculation based on gender, age range, native language, and type of employment (private, public, entrepreneur, employee, social). Prior to any apparent distinction, the first criterion was the diversity of profiles. Following this, I checked key criteria and, as the mix was objectively acceptable, I took no further action. Certainly, there are many more people who would have been interesting to include. Even so, twelve is a considerable number and it is important to remain focused. To venture a bit beyond the corporate world, I spoke to Isabelle Ferreras and Satish Kumar, and also read the work of international experts such as Michael J. Sandel, Vernā Myers, Ryan Holiday, Kay Formanek and Daniel Kahneman.

I realised I still suffered from impostor syndrome: thinking that I'm not good enough. Don't be mistaken: I know my worth, I have self-esteem. It's just that my unconscious bias is stronger than my self-confidence. It's a continuous battle, in which I admit no defeat. I told my mental parasite to go away and established that my voice was worth being heard – well, read.

It is my pleasure to present to you the twelve leaders who have partnered their voices with mine.

❝ The OPEN model is great. My first reaction was: it actually makes sense. ❞
Audrey Hanard

Audrey Hanard shares with authenticity her international management experience across the public, private, and civil society spaces.

> **Audrey Hanard** is chair of the board of directors of bpost (Belgian postal services), board member of Proximus and partner at Dalberg Global Advisors. At Dalberg, she works with her clients – who are most often international organisations, philanthropic foundations and impact investors, and governments – to improve education, employment, and health outcomes globally through designing impactful strategies in support of inclusive development. Prior to joining Dalberg, Hanard worked at the venture philanthropy firm Telos Impact, and as an engagement manager at McKinsey & Company. She is the former chair of the Friday Group, a youth think tank inspiring the Belgian public debate with innovative ideas generated through the diversity of its members.

> **❝** *I'm a big fan of your concept, because everything that you're saying is about accepting the others.* **❞**
> **Francis Blake**

Francis Blake is an example of a highly effective and humble leader who had a personal change that influenced his view on inclusion.

Married, with four children, **Francis Blake** served as the CEO and then chairman of the board of the Belgian family company Derbigum (€95 million in revenue – 350 employees). Derbigum is the leader in circular economy for the roofing industry. Derbigum is now part of the Kingspan Group. Blake is passionate about the pursuit of "Higher Purpose" as well as inspired and inspiring leadership, and new forms of organisations using the full power of collective intelligence. He is also a passionate advocate for people with disabilities, and works with his wife to change perceptions about their care and integration into the city and in life.

> " *OPEN is a nice concept and I agree with all the elements. It is true; that is what you need.* "
> **Hanan Challouki**

Hanan Challouki discusses her experiences in setting up her own company, working in the private and public sectors, while overcoming social barriers.

Hanan Challouki is passionate about the creative industry, but at the same time flabbergasted by its lack of diversity. Her mission to build a more inclusive society led her towards entrepreneurship. She developed a firm vision on marketing and communication in an extremely diverse world. Her innovative strategies landed her on the Forbes 30 Under 30 List. She started her own agency Inclusified to strategically support organisations who are dying (not literally) to become familiar with the wonderful world of diversity and inclusivity. Besides doing quite a lot of public speaking, she became an independent board member at Flanders Investment & Trade and the vice president of the Belgian Association of Marketing. She wrote her first book *Inclusieve Communicatie* (Pelckmans) in 2021, which feels to her like her paper baby.

> **" *I like OPEN; you need to be open, and it's lacking in our society culture.* "**
>
> **Ibrahim Ouassari**

The on-the-ground perspective that Ibrahim Ouassari brings is recognised by global corporations.

Ibrahim Ouassari is the founder and CEO of MolenGeek. After an atypical and self-taught career in the field of technology, he started consulting in 1999 and has become accomplished in the sector. Ouassari then left the consulting industry to embark on an entrepreneurial career with clients from the largest and most renowned companies. It was his experience that led him to launch MolenGeek in May 2015, an inclusive international technology ecosystem that makes TechWorld accessible. That's when Ouassari took on one of his biggest challenges: merging two worlds that don't meet. On the one hand, the unsuspected talents of working-class neighbourhoods and on the other hand, the world of technology.

"*You talk about openness; I talk about dignity. The terms are very close to each other. Dignity is above diversity, equality, and inclusion because it tackles the roots of discrimination.*"

Ilham Kadri

Dr Ilham Kadri is dedicated to achieving equity in the organisations she leads and to making sure that it "sticks" after she is gone.

Ilham Kadri is the CEO of Solvay and a board member at L'Oréal and A.O. Smith. She is a world citizen, a scientist, a businesswoman, and a humanist. Her international career spans more than three decades over four continents. Under her leadership at Solvay (BE), and previously at Diversey (USA), she delivered purpose-led transformations leading to sustainable and profitable businesses. Her Solvay One Planet and Solvay One Dignity roadmaps are leading to carbon neutrality before 2050, reducing inequalities at work and making diversity, equity and inclusion a business imperative.

True to her humanist values, she is an active mentor for women in STEM and founded many initiatives, such as the Hygieia Network in the USA, the Solvay Solidarity Fund, the podcast "AND is the future", and authored "Invisible Heroes" dedicated to women who clean our world. Kadri was decorated with the Légion d'honneur and received a Golden Award for the Woman of the Year in 2019. She is a Doctor Honoris Causa of the University of Namur and EWHA University. Kadri serves as a chair of the WBCSD, is a member of the Belgian Royal Academy of Sciences, of the European Round Table, and the IBC's World Economic Forum.

" *Nice! I totally agree on the empathy level, it's the E from CARE. I think it's something that is lacking today.* " **Isabel Verstraete**

With stories drawn from her personal and professional experiences, Isabel Verstraete offers a fresh and honest perspective on diversity and inclusion.

Isabel Verstraete is a seasoned brand strategy expert, author, keynote speaker, host of a business podcast, and guest lecturer at reputed institutes like Vlerick, Nyenrode Business University, VU Amsterdam and TU Delft.

During the pandemic, she researched why certain companies deal better with a crisis and discovered a pattern behind their success. She wrote a book about it: Does your brand care? Building a better world with the C A R E Principles. The C A R E Principles strategic framework helps companies create a positive impact on people and the planet and prepares organisations for the new demands of future customers and employees.

" I think it's interesting. The challenge of diversity and inclusiveness is also very much linked to organisational and societal challenges."
Isabelle Ferreras

Isabelle Ferreras challenges the OPEN way based on her work on democratising the firm.

Isabelle Ferreras is a Belgian sociologist and a political scientist. She is a senior tenured fellow of the Belgian National Science Foundation (F.N.R.S., Brussels) and a professor of sociology at the University of Louvain (Louvain-la-Neuve, Belgium) where she is affiliated with the Centre de recherches interdisciplinaires Démocratie, Institutions, Subjectivité. She is a senior research associate of the Center for Labor and a Just Economy at Harvard Law School and co-founder of the global academic network www.DemocratizingWork.org. Ferreras is a member of the Classe Technologie et Société of the Royal Academy of Sciences, Humanities and the Arts of Belgium, and former President of the Academy (2021, 2022).

> *It broadens the discussion of what it means to be a good leader. OPEN is a very pragmatic framework to create a more inclusive organisation.*
>
> **Mikaël Wornoo**

In both real-world interactions and digital ones, Mikaël Wornoo is accustomed to thinking about human interactions.

Mikaël Wornoo is one of the founders of TechWolf, an AI company helping organisations understand the skills of their workforce. Together with two friends, he started TechWolf in 2018 while studying computer science engineering. After four years, the business has raised 12M in VC funding, started working with global organisations and was recognised as Technology Pioneer by World Economic Forum.

*❝ The way you express it there is relatively close to
my point: it's about being and receiving, about
the quality of being more than anything else, more
than policies or norms or obligations. I like that level.
I think it's a right level. ❞* **Pierre Gurdjian**

As a result of Gurdjian's professional experience, a unique opportunity is presented to tap into his vast knowledge and insight into the subject.

Pierre Gurdjian is a senior professional in executive, public
sector and societal leadership and governance. He has almost three decades of experience as senior partner in strategic consulting. He is a member of the board of directors of
several leading Belgian companies and is the president of
the board of directors of the Université libre de Bruxelles. He
is the co-founder of the Belgium's 40 under 40 societal leadership development platform. He has a passion for developing leadership as a journey to purpose and wisdom.

> **"** *I congratulate you for developing a new model of profile inclusiveness and for developing capital OPEN. We need to learn to love others as they are, who they are, what they are and where they are. By accepting our differences, we participate, support, and help each other to find ourselves and love one another. So, I like your concept.* **"**
>
> **Satish Kumar**

As a humanist and universalist, Satish Kumar complements the interviewees' managerial experiences.

Peace-pilgrim, life-long activist, and former monk, **Satish Kumar** has been inspiring global change for over 50 years. He undertook a pilgrimage for peace, walking for two years without money from India to America for the cause of nuclear disarmament. Now in his 80s, Kumar has devoted his life to campaigning for ecological regeneration and social justice. He is a world-renowned author and international speaker, founder of The Resurgence Trust and editor emeritus of *Resurgence & Ecologist* – a change-making magazine he has edited for over 40 years.

" *It's nice, it's clear. It talks to me.* " **Thibaut Georgin**

Thibaut Georgin is one of those leaders who does not speak much about diversity, yet he aims to include everyone in his organisations unconditionally.

After graduating from Solvay Business School and Columbia University NY, **Thibaut Georgin** started his career as an executive at Unilever and then at bpost. In 2010, he founded the strategy consulting firm Igneos, whose mission is to assist companies and public institutions in designing and implementing strategic transformation programmes.

Throughout the past decade, he has been passionate about sustainability issues, particularly the role of companies in designing products and business models that are compatible with our finite world's limits (energy, resources, pollution, externalities).

He currently chairs the board of directors of the National Railway Company of Belgium (NMBS/SNCB) and is a board member of various organisations (ULB, Women on Board, Ecopreneur Federation). Georgin is also a visiting professor at the University of Namur and the HE2B graduate school.

" I agree with the OPEN framework;
the main story is in the nuance. "

Thierry Geerts

Inclusion is one of Thierry Geerts's core values, and he is committed to building a society that is inclusive as well as developing a sustainable business model.

Since 2011, **Thierry Geerts** has been heading Google – the company that has become much more than just a search engine – in Belgium and Luxembourg. He graduated from the VUB as a Solvay Business Engineer and soon became general manager of an industrial laundry company. With the advent of the internet in the mid-1990s, he reoriented himself towards the media industry and held various management positions at VUM (now Mediahuis), publisher of newspapers such as *De Standaard* and *Het Nieuwsblad*.

In his book *Digitalis* (2018), he describes the possibilities of the digital world. In 2021 he published his new book, *Homo Digitalis*, about the impact of the digital revolution on people and society.

Diversity, Equity, Inclusion, Inclusiveness

"Diversity and inclusion go together. Diversity is when people can show up however they are, in their multiple identities. They feel that they are contributing, bringing value, welcome to be part of the group and that's the piece about inclusion. You can have a diverse society, yet not inclusive, with siloed communities. Diversity is the sense of having safe spaces for different profiles of people. Inclusion is when you also have those people interacting, working together, and feeling part of something bigger."

Audrey Hanard

"The evolution favours diversity. In the beginning of time, at the big bang, there was no diversity. In the beginning we were all Africans; there were no other nationalities. It would be boring if we did not have this diversity; that is why I cherish and appreciate the fact of diversity and want to see no discrimination, no segregation, and no hierarchy. Organisations should welcome people of different backgrounds in the workplace. That inclusiveness creates a rich tapestry, and we can learn from each other, from different cultures, and religious traditions. We need to rise above monoculture and embrace multiculture in all workplaces."

Satish Kumar

"Diversity means to adapt yourself to the many and fast changes in society. It's to understand that what we have always learnt may not be the truth any more. It's openly daring to admit that you don't know something, which is very frightening. It's about being humbled. Inclusion and inclusiveness are about accepting that what you think and how you act might be an issue for somebody else, or might be less inviting than you reflect upon in your own head."

Isabel Verstraete

—

"In the work environment, diversity means the search for maximum insight coming from a maximum of different directions to illuminate whatever problem is at hand. In society, diversity is about making room for everyone, based on the principle of the first article of the Universal Declaration of Human Rights: every human being is equal in dignity and rights. Beyond the formal aspect of inclusion, we also have to make room for very different perspectives."

Isabelle Ferreras

—

"In business, diversity is the intention to have some people that are different in the team. It can be gender difference, origin, but also mindsets, profiles in type of management and of personality. Inclusion is about having different profiles in the management of a company. Typically, you may have different kinds of profiles but difference across levels. When it comes to taking decisions, it's still too often managed by some non-diverse people."

Thibaut Georgin

"Diversity means that everyone is different. Without diversity, the world would be very dull and very annoying. People have different characters. Inclusion is a way to put diversity into practice and to empower it. Diversity without inclusion makes no sense. Inclusion means giving people in your company with different opinions, background, and education a real safe place, where they can express their opinion and ideas that are respected and taken into consideration."

Francis Blake

—

"Diversity is the way that people can differ from each other, in any way possible. It can be the typical fourteen axes of identity, like gender, age, ethnicity and so on. But there's also just a lot of diversity in people's vision, mindsets.... Inclusion is the way that you deal with those differences. Diversity is just: you put together different people in a room, but inclusion is making it work. You can have a meeting with ten people at the table of all types of personalities and from everywhere in the world, but only the white men are feeling comfortable enough to be themselves."

Hanan Challouki

—

"Diversity is a mix of persons so that a company or an institution resembles more of society. It means integrating many facets of our society to have a broader perspective and a more global vision. It's about a diversity of culture, sexual orientation, physical disability... also a diversity of experience. Inclusion and inclusiveness is everything put in place to make sure people feel that their life and reality are considered and respected."

Ibrahim Ouassari

"Diversity and inclusion are not just concepts; they primarily are mindsets. Mindsets of Being and Receiving. In other words, the desire and curiosity to welcome other human beings in all their facets and nuances (Receiving). And the awareness of our own diversity, within ourselves (Being). This, taken together, opens a very rich space: Becoming together through Receiving the other and Being oneself."

Pierre Gurdjian

"Diversity is the beauty of humanity. Imagine if we were all the same on this planet, thinking in the same way, dressing in the same way: it would be a boring world. Nature is diverse and humankind is definitely as diverse. Modern society can only strive towards diversity. We must be sure that we have more diverse people who feel included in society and in decision-making processes, who have chances to study, to get promotions, to give their opinions. It is going further than the normal diversity topics, which is men and women and different religions. For example, in Belgium it is French and Dutch speaking or introverts and extroverts."

Thierry Geerts

"Diversity is about having an inclusive environment that gives equal opportunities to employees coming from all kinds of backgrounds, including age, gender, race, nationality, ethnicity, religion, sexual orientation, identity, ability, et cetera. I put equity and inclusion before diversity. It's about cultural change, it's about putting human dignity at the highest level. I believe that companies that put human dignity first are the ones that will stay relevant, that will last, and prosper."

Ilham Kadri

"An inclusive working environment is a welcoming working environment. Thinking about not excluding anyone is a lot easier than thinking about including anyone. Thinking about including someone is a lot harder than thinking about how to not exclude someone. Creating a more inclusive organisation is just part of being a good leader. There are a few pillars on which that is built, and inclusiveness is right up there as one of the key pillars."

Mikaël Wornoo

What wonderful ways to look at the same topic with different visions: isn't that diversity?! I do not disagree with anyone, do you? In a sense, they are all right, even if I would formulate it differently. My way of defining diversity, inclusion, inclusiveness, and equity, is the following.

Diversity is being open to different viewpoints,
patient towards differences and empathic
with people's emotions.

Equity is ensuring that everyone is treated based
on their distinctive needs.

Inclusion is using diversity to find a
safe space where everyone can be natural.
Inclusiveness is about creating this new
safe space together.

" *Doing good is good for business.* **"**
Richard Branson

Openness

You are both right. Disagreeing does not make us enemies; agreeing does not make us friends.

Openness (to someone or something) is the quality of being receptive to different ideas, opinions, or arguments, regardless of the source.

Most people consider themselves as open; what about you?

If you answer directly in the affirmative, then you are probably wrong. As we are never open enough, doubt makes you more likely to be right. If you feel you lack openness and are willing to improve, welcome to the challenge! You will be a grumpy reader if you assume you are not open and that is fine. Just don't leave; I have a perfect example for you in this chapter...

Labelling ideas

Though the exact definition of a term is not important, labelling our thoughts correctly is essential. Otherwise, how do we know we are talking about the same concept? How many times do people find themselves arguing about a word while already aligned? Language plays an important role in the process of inclusiveness, as some names reinforce mainstream choices. For instance, the use of the term "spouse" or "partner" avoids the gender representation of "husband" or "wife". "Partner" is more neutral, as it also includes non-married couples. It is important not to assume that male is neutral, particularly in the case of my maternal tongue, French, where the language structure is paternalistic. Does it mean that you will harm people if you do not use inclusive language? Certainly not. However, consider that those "minorities" may get tired of repeating "We are not married" over and over again. By not making them explain their decision, you will alleviate any experienced anxiety. For sure, thinking a bit more carefully before talking will not harm you.

———

"Everything starts with communication. Placing a label helps us to get on the same page mentally, physically, spiritually. For example, I'm not a big fan of the word feminist, but I learnt to embrace it, because it's a way to say that we need to look at women power. To remove the bias, it helps to put a name on it and to discuss it in an open, transparent, vulnerable way, to transform ourselves."
Isabel Verstraete

———

Feminism can indeed have a negative connotation, while the origins of the movement are egalitarian and humanist. It is necessary to take back ownership of the concept and not let some unpleasant experiences ruin the ideal. The same happened to me with the word diversity. I was so tired of seeing it used in a fashionable way without a deep understanding of its relevance that I decided to expel it from my dictionary. For years, I repeated, "I am not a diversity expert", while the demand for participation was high. Being reduced to the role of "the diversity girl" was annoying. "But you are the only one in the team from, you know...". Some people could not even express the words distinguishing me physically, afraid to say it wrongly, to hurt me or to be blamed. Until one day, I understood that it was not right for me to exclude a concept that was core in my private and professional life. I had to take back ownership, and if I did not agree with the way it is used, I should express my view.

"All companies and their CEOs should be proud of having diverse staff and all will be mindful of celebrating human dignity. They should transform their HR departments from Human Resources to Human Relationship. Humans are not a resource for the company, for making profit and for running business. Companies, businesses, and profit should be the resources for human dignity and wellbeing."
Satish Kumar

Changing the name of the department managing the processes of recruitment, compensation and benefits and training of your people is a positive signal internally and externally. Of course, real initiatives need to be followed in the spirit of resources transforming into relationships. Having a label that says "my company is a DEI powerhouse" may please your ego, but what does the reality look like for your employees?

"As marketers, we are used to building a brand image towards the outside world. That type of marketing is old school. If you want to be a relevant brand, then start your efforts internally. If not, don't start shouting it externally."
Isabel Verstraete

I have often been surprised when attending awards events aimed at congratulating some companies' efforts. Generally, there is no diversity in terms of background: all studied at prestigious universities, had connections before entering the workforce, followed the same career path, and... are primarily white. I have observed on too many occasions that the jury members complimented themselves for the diversity of nominees: one third were women. The fact that one third of the nominees are female is not an excellent achievement. It may be a significant step forward, but it is still not a success. For the most part, those women have the same background as two-thirds of men. Secondly, women are not diversity, they are mixity. Women are not a minority in terms of population: in 2021, they represented 49.6% of the world[4], 51.1% of the European and 50.7% of the Belgian population[5]. When they are underrepresented at levels of power as a minority group, the dynamics of exclusion vary. There is no man who can say, "I never met a woman". However, there are many people who have never encountered anyone from a minority background (origin, socioeconomic...). Including those you do not know is more difficult than including those you do.

Today we see an effervescence of awards, for which criteria and jury choices are not clear. As the jury composition will determine the bias of the decisions, the selection process must be as transparent and inclusive as possible. Furthermore, these awards may be seen as the culmination of all the efforts, but that's not really the point. A prize cannot be the objective. Thibaut Georgin takes it further by questioning whether diversity should even be the goal.

"Diversity shouldn't be a goal; it's an enabler. It's not something to be done because it's compulsory, fashionable, or a moral obligation. I strongly believe that diversity is the way to move in the direction of sustainability."
Thibaut Georgin

I do believe that Diversity, Equity, Inclusion (DEI), is a moral obligation, but translated into business language, one will talk about performance. When I was raising funds for my non-profit organisation, I had several presentations deck: one for public institutions, a second for companies, a third for public foundations, a fourth for private foundations, and even a fifth for the social sector. The content was the same, but the way it was presented and the language used was different. Having a foot in each of those worlds, I learnt to comprehend their sensibilities. This first professional story of Thierry Geerts is linked to his ability to talk to everyone.

"When I graduated from university, I did an internship in a company that wanted to hire me. Their reason was, "You seem to be able to talk to everyone." I would have imagined arguments like "your brilliance", "your skills", "you are amazing" or whatever. Today, everyone should have open conversations at all levels and reach out to people that are sometimes not reached."
Thierry Geerts

Today DEI is a fashionable topic, but this may not always serve the cause, as the "why" risks becoming entangled with the "how". Labels are of course nice for employee motivation, they help your brand, and if you are doing good in your society and for your employees, you will have the means to do better. Just don't fall into the trap Pierre Gurdjian is referring to – a risk I alas experienced in some organisations.

"Inclusiveness should never become 'boxed in' within the boundaries of formal ESG frameworks and processes. It is much more than adhering to norms and standards. It has to become woven into the fabric of the culture of the organisation."
Pierre Gurdjian

Openness & personality

I was surprised to see openness as part of a personality test. You might say, "It's normal; openness is a quality that some have to a greater extent than others." Maybe. I am concerned, however, that some presentations refer to openness as an attribute of extroverts, while introverts are considered closed. Openness is portrayed as having a positive correlation with imagination, creativity, emotion, adventure... That can induce a dangerous conclusion such as: artists are open while accountants are not. That is simply not true. An open mind is not confined to a particular personality; rather, it transcends all. I have found more openness in a finance director, loving rigid procedures and risk averse, than in a painter, however creative he was. What is true is that the more open you are to the world, the more things you will perceive. The *Scientific American*[6] journal states that, "Studies show that open people are less susceptible to the psychological 'blind spots' that help us pare back the complexity of the world. And research shows that this characterization is more than a metaphor: open people literally see things differently in terms of basic visual perception." In a metro, some passengers notice everything that is occurring, while others are so focused on their phones that they miss their stop (it has happened to me when reading... and not just once...).

There is one nuance that I would like to add to this: openness can be a temporary condition. A person may be in a different frame of mind depending on the time of day. In the morning, people are often busy preparing for the day, so less open to their surroundings, while in the evening, they are more attentive to what is happening around them.

A personal preference may lead one to be more or less open, so evolving is possible. It is human nature. The potential to improve depends on the degree of openness you can maintain based on your natural posture. The ability to be open is a state of mind that is developed through appropriate training and healthy working relationships. Detecting blind spots requires continuous observation and learning.

" *There is a Field between right and wrong; meet me there.* **"** **Rumi**

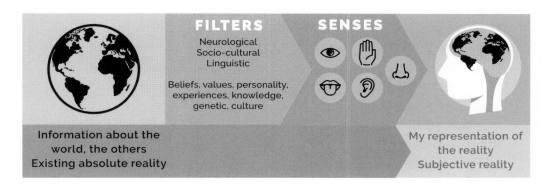

The truth is that... there is no absolute truth. I like the notion of world maps in Neuro-linguistic programming[7], outlining that there is no absolute truth, only relative truth. It all starts there. The received information goes through all our filters and our senses before being felt and expressed by us. The interpretation of the same information will vary in function for each of us.

If you are convinced by an idea, that's awesome. It does not mean that the idea is right. It is right *for you*. This nuance is game changing.

People generally think they are open. Until... difference comes too close. A man says he is okay working with and even befriending foreigners, but if his daughter wants to marry a black man... "That's different." Kids are taught to respect other cultures, but they are discouraged from altering their way of life. Children are generally perceived as a continuation of ourselves. The same kind of reasoning applies to our employees. Often, managers assume their methods are the same as those of their team members, whether this refers to daily work or specific events. Have you already thought, for example, that choosing a location, food, and drink is not neutral? Neither is the type of activity and associated noise level. Every one of your employees has his or her own sensitivity, likes and dislikes, personality...

As soon as I join a team for the first time, I ask what communication tools are used. Often, there is no structural framework. The request I always make is the same: regardless of the tool, you should have one, and the choice should be collective. Some find it intrusive to have the application on the phone, while others need it in order to quickly record any thinking. What solution to choose? One where notifications can be shut down during specific hours (or permanently). As long as everyone is willing to put in an effort, there will always be a way. Begin by examining the need, then the method, and finally the mix of solutions. I am adaptable to a wide range of tools, and I have used most of them: they all have both pros and cons. Some swear by only one: I decided this battle was not worth fighting, so I follow the flow. When I collaborate with different teams, I sometimes use three distinct tools: that is okay. Does it mean that I am easy to work with? Not necessarily. Anything related to my freedom makes me intransigent. Do not ask me (as a previous manager did) to report working hours or record what I did, how I did it and when. Although I am extremely open-minded regarding tools, I remain extremely closed-minded regarding control reports (and I worked in finance…). So, what do you say, am I open or not?

I asked Satish Kumar if there was a specific moment when he realised, "Oh, that's diversity!".

"I spoke in many universities, mostly in Berlin, New York, and Tokyo. I found universities had a more diverse population of students, who get along with one another better than in many companies. Young people appear to be less prejudiced but when they get into businesses, they are forced to practise discrimination due to the corporate culture. Therefore, corporations should learn from universities."
Satish Kumar

Having discovered diversity at university, this statement resonates with me. My world suddenly expanded to encompass people from many different backgrounds, as well as possibilities for the future. In fact, I spent the first four months conversing with people along "Paul Egée", the street situated in the middle of the

Université Libre de Bruxelles. Failures in exams and loss of pride were the costs, but meeting people is never regrettable.

Not all my friends made it to the second year. Even though no direct discriminating criteria were in place (the exams and scores were the same for everyone), many of my friends who failed were from ethnic minorities. Their defeatism was the most disturbing aspect of their reaction. It felt like this delicious dream of graduating from a prestigious business school was too much for somebody *like them*. But that was considered okay, because they had tried. They moved to other faculties, where students who look like them are more used to achieving success. Fortunately, the situation has become a little bit better now, as I see more diversity in the graduates. Unfortunately, the diversity present in education tends to fade as you rise, in terms of types of studies and, later, type of jobs.

BCG and Google joined forces to perform a study[8] in 2022, concluding that, "*Without action, CEO roles will continue to be occupied by white men... Based on education, we would expect six times more women in CEO roles.*" 56% of master's degrees are awarded to women, while only 11% of women are on boards. They deep dive into the choice of studies and "*Neither does choice of field of study fully explain such disparity, as women also represent 35–40% of the more specialised degrees in Economics and STEM.*"

The academic world is mainly male dominated. Isabelle Ferreras knows it too well.

"*I reflect on academia as a very non-inclusive sector, and that's a shame because today more women graduate than men. The highest ranks in professorship are still heavily male-dominated, and it's not providing for the most excellent type of organisations. Women are excellent, but they are barred, not capable of advancing as fast as men. In Europe in particular, universities and research institutions should massively reorganise themselves to make inclusiveness possible.*"
Isabelle Ferreras

Been seen

My entry into the professional world was like a jump into another world. I did not encounter many people of whom I thought, "Wow, she or he is really open". In general, the tendencies are either paternalistic or maternalistic. "I accept you because I will save you. Now answer my many questions. Actually, no matter your answers, I will not reconsider my clichés." These are the unspoken words that I felt many times. One director was a promising exception. While working in her team for three months, a colleague mentioned me as "the woman with the veil". She said: "Who?" He insisted "the woman with the veil". It was unclear to her who he was referring to. After a few minutes of misunderstanding, it finally became apparent to her that he was alluding to me. She was shocked. The fact that I was covering my hair had never been observed by her. It was offensive to her that someone would speak so disparagingly about another individual. "It's not like it isn't visible," he said, surprised that she did not notice it. "I see her personality and her skills," she replied. "The rest does not matter." There are no words to describe how I felt. I was free in her eyes. Free from judgment, free from bad looks, free from staring.

———

I was not the woman in a veil,
I was seen for my personality and skills.

———

This contrasted with an incident that had occurred in the same location a few weeks earlier. I stayed late at work; remember what I said about imposter syndrome combined with constant pressure to achieve excellence and a passion for my work – this made me an ideal candidate for systemic overtime. As I was walking to the restrooms, a man expressed his displeasure about the cleaning chariot blocking his path. I wondered why he was sharing his frustration with me: we did not know one another. He glared at me for some moments, and then explained, somewhat exasperated by my lack of reaction, that I must put my things away. It took me a few seconds to understand. In his mind, I was a cleaning lady, even though the staff had their own uniforms, and I was wearing a silk dress. To annoy him, I put on my disapproving face (with some years of theatre experience, you can play anyone at will) and replied, "Maybe you can do it. This way you will be useful," and I left. I was hurt. In no way did I feel offended by the fact that he thought I was cleaning; I consider all workers and believe that many valuable jobs are not sufficiently respected (just think of how reliant you are on your housekeeper or babysitter when they are not available). It was painful to realise that despite my education, diploma, prestigious-branded clothes, and employment, he believed a woman *like me* can only be in an office for a cleaning job.

Do you see the difference? She was open, he was not. In the same workplace. Their creativity or otherwise does not enter the balance. It depends on many things: education, socio-economic background, neighbourhood, family and friends, interests... and, of course, goodwill.

> **"** *It's hard to be humble, when you're as great as I am.* **"**
> **Muhammad Ali**

The right ego

The question one must ask is this: is your daily life sufficiently diverse to allow you to consider yourself open? Being open with your peers who think and look like you will not help you grow. How can you understand your degree of openness?

Openness is a matter of personal and professional development, and it will not come without a fight with your worst enemy: yourself, and without the support of your best ally: yourself.

> **"** *By removing the ego – even temporarily – we can access what's left standing in relief. By widening our perspective, more comes into view.* **"**
> **Ryan Holiday[9]**

Our egos are generally responsible for our closed mindsets. "My opinion is the best. My company is the best. My civilisation is the best." You may feel that you are doing well, even great. However, using the superlative places you above, establishing a hierarchy in which others or other ways are directly underneath. If others are not good enough, what is the point of listening? It would be far better to simply tell them what they should do to become as great as you are. Isn't that so?

Openness induces accepting that you can both be right, in your own way.

———

"Pay attention to these structural dynamics that make it possible or otherwise for anyone to be open. It is not only an individual preference; it also reflects some sort of collective capitalisation that the organisation is providing to individuals. If you're talking about someone and her manager, keep in mind that the manager is always 'more right' than the n-1; because the manager is in a position to subordinate the other person."
Isabelle Ferreras

———

In every relationship where there is a power balance, ego can be an obstacle to openness. It is the same for managers and employees as for parents and children. If you are in a position of authority, it will be a challenge to consider that other opinions are as good as yours, or even better...

———

"As a leader, you must identify when your ego is important to use and when you need to put it on the side. When I sold our company, I wanted to have my picture in the newspaper, but the buyers desired to be 'discreet'. At the end, the customers don't care, nothing changes for them. That was my ego being in the way. I would have liked to be recognised, but what does it really change? Do I need it?

The problem is when your ego takes too much importance versus the good of the organisation. I know someone who is changing the name of a big company just to make sure that he can put his own name on something. It is not creating value; it is a waste of time, energy, and motivation for the teams."

Francis Blake

Does this story remind you of someone you know? Well, this individual is not the only one. Many reorganisations have been realised with the aim of giving more power to one, a stamp to a director, a sense of making a mark. Most of the time, those leaders do not even realise that their reasons are purely egocentric.

Francis Blake confesses to nearly falling into the trap. It takes a lot of courage to realise that, while an action might be gratifying to oneself, it is not necessary for others. I too have had a lot of moments when I wanted to share my accomplishments on social media; "Look at this young woman, how I helped her. And this guy, I took him from a bad neighbourhood to succeed in one of the best schools." You see those kinds of posts that show false humility – "I only helped a bit; the merit goes to the team" – while casting a shadow over the colleagues and even the company. What does this exposure bring to the person concerned? Nothing. With social media, one must pay much more attention to stay focused on the why of one's actions. There is a difference between communicating with purpose and showing off, which can corrupt the purpose and trigger a loss of credibility. It is true for a personality and for a brand: think about the right balance for your communication.

" *Let's be clear: competitiveness is an important force in life…. Only you know the race you're running. That is, unless your ego decides the only way you have value is if you're better than, have more than, everyone everywhere.* "
Ryan Holiday[10]

There is more validity in this sentiment when applied to a collective. We know that saying, "I am the best" is not really acceptable (except in certain occupations where arrogance is valued; no further comment). However, "We are the best" …well, it's widely acknowledged. The acceptance of group hierarchies within a society is dangerous. Societal inequalities are based on these assumptions, which, when set against a background of economic difficulties, can lead to conflict. The belief becomes reality if repeated sufficiently, and we can even see proof of this.

What did I tell you?
Women can't drive. No sexism
here, just the facts. On my way here,
someone blocked the whole road just to
park. Guess what it was? A woman! She did not
know how to park. I pushed the horn just once,
and told her nicely to hurry up. Her excuse was that
it's hard to park on the left. Pfft, they are so limited.
Do what you can: take care of the kids, cook for
your husband. Go home! And the crazy girl yelled
at me! Completely hysterical. They just can't
handle the truth. Men are better than them.
Yeah, I had some doubts, but now I'm
convinced. Let's keep power.

Although this scene is a cliché, it is still very real. When you are strongly convinced of something, the universe will show you that it is true. You don't have to believe me; it's just physics.

> **"** *Everything is energy and that's all there is to it. Match the frequency of the reality you want, and you cannot help but get that reality. It can be no other way. This is not philosophy. This is physics.* **"**
>
> **Albert Einstein**

Reality is physics

You can only see what you want to see, and there is no reality to it. It is disturbing, right? The next time someone says, "I believe in what I see", respond by stating that even what she or he sees cannot be trusted. The reaction should be funny.

You can only see what you want to see, and there is no reality to it.

Stereotypes are difficult to eliminate once they have become established. Until it becomes a major threat not only to yourself, but also to your company's performance and peace. How can you incorporate the ideas of people who you perceive as being beneath you? A company where people manage their ego may transform into a hub for new and disruptive ideas, since everyone will be aware that no idea is better than the next.

As a CEO, Francis Blake shared how diversity has boosted their creativity for better performance.

"Some of the most brilliant and creative evolutions were ideas coming from machine operators who could hardly read and write. They were helped by others to write a suggestion on something that seemed crazy. Then we believed in it, we tested it, and results were incredible. Our engineers calculated that the best result possible for waste reduction was 1%: we reached 0.6%. Because we managed to use the collective intelligence, we could beat a lot of expectations. Everyone had fun."
Francis Blake

Having fun while improving productivity thanks to full inclusiveness of all employees, no matter their education and hierarchical level: this is music to my ears.

When I was twenty-seven years old, I was promoted to the position of head of a department with ten employees, all older than me (apart from one), all male (except one: the management assistant). The succession was natural since I had co-created the department and made it grow with the previous manager. Some individuals found the process difficult. Despite admitting that I was the right person for the job, a man declared that he could not work for *someone like me*. The statement was made privately, of course; he expressed his intention to deny everything if I repeated it, and he was confident of his predominance. The thought of reporting him crossed my mind. His threat intimidated me, but I was mostly annoyed by the idea (imagined or real) that management might say: "Another story from her." There was no actual story, but due to my imposter syndrome, I felt it was necessary to keep a low profile. In my head, the sentence "Be happy you are employed and well treated" resonated. His sexist, racist, and homophobic mentality was well known: he could not resist making jokes that only he found amusing. Though a powerful tool for deconstructing stereotypes, humour can also serve to perpetuate them. My ego could have governed my actions and I could have fired him. Well, noting his seniority in the company and the conditions of his comfortable contract, the human resource partner would have placed him in internal mobility, enabling employees to remain on payroll for certain months until they find a new function. Instead, my stubbornness led me to a different course of action. The situation turned into a personal challenge: I had to make him recognise my skills, my leadership, and my humanity. Furthermore, I was pragmatic: a team member leaving shortly after my appointment would have created a negative impression.

I was not hurt by his frank revelation; I had learned resilience the hard way. Even though I despised what he represented, I persuaded him to stay on the team for a couple of months, with a very practical informal deal: I could give him positive or negative references, which he knew the importance of. We had a strange relationship. There was no denying that we did not like each other, and that was fine with us. We were able to work together seamlessly: our personalities were perfectly compatible. While he loved chatting and getting all the gossip, I was much more task-oriented (something that evolved over time), so he had access to a wealth of information that was crucial for the type of work I performed. We even shared some complicit laughs at times. I recognise, when I reflect on this, that despite his narrow-mindedness, he acted in a very professional manner. That couldn't have been easy. As time passed, I grew to respect him professionally. A colleague asked me: "How can you respect this man, after everything he has done to you?" My reply was, "I respect him because I respect myself." Respecting others is about respecting oneself.

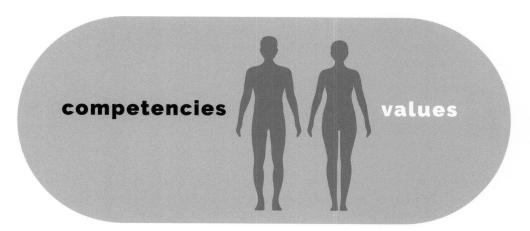

Also, accepting contradiction helps. Being raised in a family with a disparity of opinions made it easy for me to understand. If it's not that intuitive for you, try to work on it. See the bright side of adversity. Besides, compartmentalising is useful: on the one hand, the individual with his personal values and experiences; on the other hand, the colleague with his qualifications and... let's admit it, his utility – don't we have contract of mutual usefulness between an employer and employee? In the centre, one human being. Same personality, same person, but a different perspective. Embrace the fact that you do not need to really like your co-worker. Don't be concerned if you do not share all values. Do not be afraid of contradiction; rather, celebrate its acceptance. The absence of it should be your concern. This is undoubtedly tiring. However, life would be very dull without it.

Whenever you are in a position of authority – whether you are a manager, a parent, a teacher... – there is a strong temptation to make decisions and then let others carry them out.

We should be open to all human beings even if their attitudes are not acceptable to us. Of course, this limitation should not be exceeded – a limit being a crime[11].

"There is a joint responsibility as a society to drive progress. I'm all for openness; however, living together also means that there are some boundaries that we jointly need to agree on, which are extremely tough to define. For example, if someone says 'Paedophilia is okay' or 'Remove freedom of speech': are you willing to even start debating it? What's the minimum level of common agreement to be able to live together? A common respect for boundaries set by fundamental legal texts such as the Constitution should be one of them."
Audrey Hanard

In spite of the necessity of setting a limit to openness, determining it collectively is almost impossible. And if done, we tend to soon forget about it. Several years after I co-established Talented Youth Network (TYN), Chaima, a former student who became a volunteer in charge of a training programme, approached Yasmina, the coordinator, and requested that a specific course be offered. Following my instructions, Yasmina replied that the course is part of another training programme, and that it cannot be mixed. The structure must be followed. Chaima refused to accept the answer and argued for several days. Yasmina, a very patient person, asked, "Why are you so insistent? It's not only my view; even Ihsane agrees with me." Chaima responded, "It's you who told us to never accept an answer if we don't agree, and to fight for our ideas." I fell out of my chair when I heard this. Chaima was completely right: we teach principles and then are annoyed when things do not turn out our way. Parents will recognise this kind of story. Do we not feel proud when our teenagers stand up for their rights externally, but angry when our position is challenged? The same holds true for all relationships that begin with a difference in status. A mentor with a mentee, a parent with their children, a manager with his or her staff... There is an inherent sense of superiority, which must be overcome to listen and adapt.

Thierry Geerts is deeply concerned while enthusiastic about our language difference in Belgium.

"Few fights are worth fighting. We must learn to disagree without fighting. In Belgium, French and Dutch speakers do not disagree about everything: 80% of the things, they agree on. So instead of talking about the 20%, let's talk about the 80%. Depolarising the discussion is probably the number one challenge. If you have one extremist against the other, then they will never be able to have a discussion. While if we go to the roots, then you can agree with most of the people."

Thierry Geerts

Find what we have in common, for instance, setting our values with a combined bottom-up and top-down approach. The process can be applied in any organisation and even in society in general. The risk is agreeing on a term while the understanding is different, or disagreeing on a formulation while the understanding is the same. In both cases, one needs to spend enough times aligning (what can be aligned) with pedagogy and accepting that one needs to leave room to disagree. To be receptive to other opinions, one needs to respect and feel respected. Respect is a common shared value. In many trainings and coaching, participants complaint about not being respected enough. Do they mean the same thing?

Social beings

I once intervened in a conflict between two colleagues. According to one, greeting your team members is an essential part of the morning routine. As for the other, she found it important not to be disturbed. Could you imagine the problem? He was shocked every morning that she did not say "Hello, how are you?" (with, as a bonus, a kiss). She was irritated by him for interrupting her just to ask, "How are you?" She thought he was not respecting her. He thought she was not respecting him. Both were moaning about the same missing value. The concrete expression of the value is different for each of them, for each one of us. How often have you found yourself complaining about a lack of respect, love, attention, esteem, or consideration? Is there anyone who denies the importance of those values? The degree of self-confidence you possess does not matter. Feeling valued is essential for everyone. Sometimes it can be difficult to recognise it since our worst friend, the ego, places many obstacles in our way. As social creatures, human beings rely on one another for survival. In the 1960s, American psychologist Harry Harlow conducted a famous study[12] on baby monkeys kept in complete isolation for two years. The goal was to analyse the impact of maternal separation. The poor animals showed social deficits with symptoms such as social withdrawal, "rocking back and forth, hitting and biting themselves, and running away from any approaching monkey". Those results confirmed what we are accustomed to thinking of as natural today: that the parent-child bond plays a crucial role in healthy development and that social privation has permanent consequences. The scandal linked to Romanian orphans[13] in the 1990s is even more scary: "Children were getting adequate food, hygiene and medical care, but had woefully few interactions with adults, leading to severe behavioural and emotional problems."[14]

We are those babies. Throughout our lives, we need love, support, and encouragement. It took me some time to come to terms with that. I always thought: "I don't care what others think, I don't need compliments." Though the level of self-esteem and sensitivity may vary, there is no question about the necessity. No matter whether you are a CEO, an executive, a director, entrepreneur, manager... you need social recognition. You value others' opinions. Even if you made a lot of effort to become less susceptible to others, it remains. The key is to listen to all opinions, not just those you admire or trust. For that, you need to have those people inside your company, therefore your recruitment process should include diversity in all its steps. The impression that you are a good listener may be true, but if the people you surround yourself with are not diverse enough, then your listening skills are likely to be fruitless.

"In order to ensure that our society has enough diversity we have to be colour blind and not look for divisions in the name of religion, nationality or race. We are one humanity, and our unity and diversity dance together. They are complementary."
Satish Kumar

Profiles puzzle

I always say that I could not stand working with me. It is not that I don't like myself, but my character cannot be combined with a similar character for a long period of time. The result would be chaotic and self-destructing. Each time I wanted to create a new organisation, I looked for partners who have a different personality and background. When I hire new employees, I seek complementarity above all. The profile description is written according to what is missing. As part of my initial recruitment efforts, I have even asked candidates to take a personality test (voluntary, not mandatory) or to share the results if they had already taken one. In time, I became adept at analysing profiles directly during an interview. The detected profile is compared with the existing team members. When I am working with highly organised people, I will look for someone who is flexible (disorganised). If they are stressed, I would favour someone who is not afraid of being late. As a result, even what is considered a personal fault may be turned into an asset. The effort must be permanent as the natural tendency is to recruit someone who looks and thinks like you. It is not intuitively incorrect; it is just a matter of bias.

Therefore, your recruitment team needs to be trained to analyse their own unconscious bias and to think in complementary terms rather than of similarity. Do not hesitate to challenge the recruiting team about the type of candidates missing for a function: is it a reflection of the market, or is it structurally this way as a bias on their part? Do not be confrontational with them: human nature is suspicious, and that is what has helped us survive for so long. Learning to let go of our instinct of fearing a difference is necessary in order to embrace evolution at the workplace. It does not mean that all my recruitments were successful, but at least we never lacked diversity. Unfortunately, I had to fire some people. It broke my heart (and my neck) the first time. Then, I understood that keeping an unhappy person for a job not well done neither helps the person, nor the organisation. Which does not mean that the decision is easy: putting someone out of a job is a disgrace, socially and economically. I do not believe that they are bad workers... just the wrong profile at the wrong place at the wrong moment. It is best to help them figure out where they can be happier and use our network to find the right place: in the best cases, it happens quickly; in other cases, it takes more time...

"We provide assessment and development programmes, including training sessions, for leaders to grow and nurture an inclusive mindset. I was trained with my team on unconscious bias, which is very important because when you interview, you don't realise you have your own bias – it's part of you. So how do we catch it? We build a culture in which individuals feel empowered to speak up when they experience or witness a non-inclusive behaviour. Back in 2019, I launched a 'Code of Business Integrity' where there is zero tolerance for discrimination. We hire and fire for that, so people know it is a strong value."
Ilham Kadri

As a humble leader, Francis Blakes recognises his mistakes in hiring people who look like him.

"I made many mistakes in my career. I started employing people that were similar to me: 'This guy, I can relate to him. We are going to work nicely together.' After two or three failures, I started to change and employ people who were bringing something else. It's easier when you have all your people thinking the same way, but then if one thinks it is a good idea to jump off the cliff, everybody is going to jump. You need someone who will see another way to get down than to jump."
Francis Blake

Mikaël Wornoo had an interesting experience when recruiting for his brand-new company: even if he paid attention to diversity, there was a forgotten criterion.

"We were proud that we were only looking at missing skills and complementarity. After, we checked: everybody was around the same age, 25 years old. This was an important lesson. You might think you're creating a diverse group, but because of some bias, you might essentially be creating a very homogenised group. It is still about business performance: what are the dimensions of diversity for my company and how can these be equally represented in the business?"
Mikaël Wornoo

Mikaël Wornoo has used his own experience to improve his fieldwork. Indeed, he co-created a company using artificial intelligence for recruitment. He was inspired by his favourite book, the international bestseller *Thinking, Fast and Slow* from Daniel Kahneman[15], a Nobel Prize winner in Economic Sciences. The empirical findings of Kahneman and his colleagues challenge the assumption of human rationality prevailing in modern economic theory. He established a cognitive basis for common human errors that arise from heuristics and biases[16], and developed prospect theory[17]. Daniel Kahneman wrote: *"Freely mixing metaphors, we have in our head a remarkably powerful computer, not fast by conventional hardware standards, but able to represent the structure of our world by various types of associative links in a vast network of various types of ideas. The spreading of activation in the associative machine is automatic, but we have some ability to control the search of memory, and also to program it so that the detection of an event in the environment can attract attention."[18]*

By not paying attention, your previous recruitments determine the new ones, as a repeatable pattern.

"The human brain tends to simplify tasks by taking shortcuts, which can lead to logical errors. When recruiting, using software that utilises artificial intelligence can inadvertently perpetuate existing biases. For example, if a company only has a history of hiring male engineers, the algorithm will be less likely to recommend female candidates. To avoid this, it is important to ensure that the dataset used to train the algorithm is diverse and not disproportionately skewed towards some group, so as not to reinforce existing biases in the hiring process."
Mikaël Wornoo

If it is hard to attract people bringing diversity, the lack of inclusion will drive them away. A constant watch should be performed to ensure that attracted talents do not quit because of the internal atmosphere.

"At Google, we have representatives for diverse groups helping to understand what the inclusivity problems of different communities are (black community or Muslim community or...) Equity is to be sure that everybody is paid and promoted in the same way, and that voices are heard. If you don't have this equity part, people will quit."
Thierry Geerts

The idea of identifying representatives is interesting, although they should not be considered as a spokesperson for their communities. Their role is there to bring ideas, first as human beings, then with one part of their many identities. Obviously, a community will also have diversity in its pool. I feel I need to emphasise this as sometimes people ask me a question, then they assume that I answer for all women, or all Muslims, or… I only represent myself.

___

If it is hard to attract people bringing diversity, the lack of inclusion will drive them away.

___

Unequal needs

The OPEN way places a great deal of emphasis on opinion, like a process composed of different activity boxes. Receptivity to other opinions requires the presence of one's own thoughts. Otherwise, the reaction will either result in complete rejection or in blind acceptance. Nevertheless, beliefs do not define us: they are not what make us who we are. We are not our opinions. Generally, we believe that our thoughts represent our identity and then, out of pride, we cling to them as if they were our soul's guarantee. "If I accept this, then what's next?" What's next is that you will evaluate each situation when it occurs. By accepting that a woman will take lactation pauses, it does not mean that anyone will demand an additional break. Thanks to the confinements caused by Covid-19, we have already seen that the practice of homeworking benefits both employers and employees. Although some adjustments were necessary, companies were not forced to implement a sustainable change due to a specific requirement. As soon as a need arises, take into consideration its context and circumstances. A comprehensive approach should be adopted, taking into account all types of concerns. Because of the evolution of opinion regarding homeworking, the companies' identity did not change. Boards of directors did not suddenly revise their why, linked to a change in the how. As individuals, as a group and as a company, our opinions evolve. It is not a sign of weakness. It is a sign of openness.

___

Boards of directors did not suddenly revise their why, linked to a change in the how.

___

Human resources departments created rules for homeworking based on the types of jobs, not based on individual profiles. A rule was devised and implemented. Several risks were detected primarily depending on the personality profile of the employee. Individual appearance was not relevant to determining those risks: it all came down to the inclusiveness of profiles.

> "Hybrid working makes it very easy for someone working remotely to feel excluded by the conversation. We have policies at the company, especially when sharing key moments: everybody knows about it, not only the people in the office. Those observations hold equally for people of colour, with disabilities, not speaking the main language, LGBT+... An inclusive workplace is always going to be better if you don't have to park a part of yourself to fit in."
> **Mikaël Wornoo**

Each employee faces a different set of challenges. Although introverts may find homeworking easy for a short period of time, they are likely to be overburdened by their intrinsic nature. The act of going to work allows one to make face-to-face contact with others when taking a coffee break, going to lunch, or even just using the restroom. If someone has trouble speaking up in a meeting, physical distance will make it even more difficult. A colleague told me that with online meetings, he thinks more before talking. "I will raise the hand only if I really need to say something and nobody has said it before." Fewer jokes, fewer comments, less spontaneity.

A person who is an extrovert might find homeworking difficult at first, but he or she will be more likely to contact colleagues "just to chat" as time goes on. The creative mind can have trouble adjusting to a lack of social interaction, space, or hearing other people's ideas. As the risks are not the same, you cannot define a single strategy based solely on your understanding of the situation. For any transition to be successful, all profiles must be embraced. Accept that some people speak more easily (and more loudly), and others wait politely for the microphone to be handed over. Corporate culture favours extrovert approaches: the person who speaks the most will be heard. As an example, daring is often a value embedded in a company's values. Extroverts are more prone to dare since their energy is primarily external. Consequently, as a leader, it is your responsibility to assist introverts in becoming successful. It is important to manage with equity, not equality: some require more encouragement. Having the same attitude towards all your employees will not make you fair. On the contrary, you will be unfair by ignoring specific needs. A widely known image shows three children watching a game with their father.

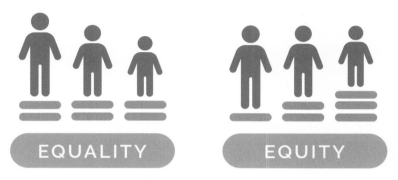

When the father provides more boxes for a small child, equity is created. The why is of utmost importance.

Why are they there? To watch the game (without buying tickets apparently).

What is the problem? The children cannot see.

What is needed? Supporting boxes. Oh, here are three!

How to allocate them? One for the eldest, two for the youngest, none for the grown-up man.

Is this discrimination? No. This is equity.

A discriminatory act would be to refuse to provide two boxes to another child on the grounds that "She is a girl; football games are not appropriate for girls." The difference is straightforward. If some people require accommodation, you must make sure that all people in the same situation are able to access it. Review all privileges and benefits offered by your organisation: do all employees have equal access to them? You cannot just say "Only for you." Adaptation must be based on specific needs justified by a different context. This is not an exception. It is a flexible and fair rule. Unjustified exceptions create tension between the *privileged* and the *common* workers.

When I started working, I was following a finance management traineeship: that means that every six months, I had a changing role in a different department in the finance environment. An opportunity was presented to me to expatriate to Budapest, an experience that I shared previously. Most young professionals were eager to travel to foreign countries. Except that the rule specified that finance trainees could only be posted to countries in the "Benedelux area": Belgium (obviously), the Netherlands, Germany, Luxembourg. Well, Budapest is outside this. I still managed to get there, because of exceptional and justified circumstances (I had experience on the project), but as no explanation was officially communicated, it was perceived as neither equality nor equity. My fellow trainees were jealous; I was happy. For once, I was on the other side (which still does not make the situation fairer).

Colleagues should accept, acknowledge, and even celebrate differences among themselves. Yes, celebrate the uniqueness! You do not have to hide your special needs; those add a richness to your life and to that of your workmates. Let's take the example of food: have you ever held or participated in an event where people were invited to bring their favourite dishes? Isn't it marvellous to see all that diversity? Just… a word of caution: please do not make the mistake of assuming that a Moroccan will bring couscous. Really, it happened to me, and the party became a nightmare. Some people were extremely disappointed (and expressed it verbally and non-verbally) to see me arrive with a dish of pasta bolognese. The shock was contagious. I did not even know what to say. This is one of my favourite dishes! I do not know how to make couscous; I love eating it, of course. Was it not part of the game to discover new things about your colleagues, to go beyond stereotypes? One even said to me, "I promised my wife I would bring home some of your couscous!" "Did I say I would make couscous?" "No, but come on, you are Moroccan, not Italian!" I responded, "I honestly deliberated between mussels and Belgian fries (sorry to remind you that they are not French but Belgian fries) and spaghetti bolognese". The most offensive reaction was from another colleague: she did not believe me. As she saw it, I was just playing unmarginalised because I wanted to be a part of the group. "You know, you can have your own favourite meal; there is no shame in it." I answered, "But I know it is okay! Why don't you just accept that it is not couscous!" She glanced at me with a maternal look: "One day, you will get there, you will feel it." This comment silenced me. The festivity was ruined. I felt so let down (my pasta was delicious, though). Even at an event called "a multicultural lunch", the room was filled with persistent clichés. Not from everybody, of course. As usual, hurtful reactions are more visible.

Please do not be discouraged by my experience. You may use it as a gentle warning. I still believe that such events are valuable. Just make sure that your people are aware beforehand. Train them. Too much focus is put on compliance with must-have boxes: "multicultural lunch, check". I know for a fact that the lunch was reported as a success. It was not. Did they really care? It is a pity because most of the work is seen in terms of budget, time and energy. When the centre piece of your puzzle is missing, it is no use building it before locating the missing part. It may be permanently lost. Some companies are hesitant to take risks in this regard: it is true that some have suffered negative publicity in the past because of their daring advertising campaigns. If your sole objective is to protect your company's brand, then all action will be tainted by self-protection. There will be resistance to what is said and done, which will result in actions that may produce a flattering image but have minimal impact. You do not need to believe in karma to recognise that an empty facade cannot be sustained, not even in terms of corporate branding. At a networking event, a director shared a valuable piece of advice: "You have a clear vision, which you express loudly and flawlessly. Of course, people will criticise you. You will never have unanimity. But who has? Maybe only the silent ones please everybody. But they are not respected. So, you had better get used to it."

" *Let yourself be open and life will be easier.*
A spoon of salt in a glass of water makes the water
undrinkable. A spoon of salt in a lake is almost
unnoticed. **"** **Buddha Siddhartha Gautama Shakyamuni**

As a follow-up to the experience shared in the introduction, it may be useful to ask all your employees what their constraints are before organising any major event. The existence of other celebration days for minority groups should be acknowledged. Jewish employees may want to take leave on Rosh HaShanah and Yom Kippur and even Chanukah; Muslims, on Eid-al-Fitr, Eid-al-Adha, Ramadan, and even Muharram; Hindus, on Diwali and Navaratri; and some, for their kids' birthdays. While it is understandable that additional holidays will not be granted for every employee's celebration, refusing those specific days off should not be an option. Working on a day that is of significance to an individual constitutes a form of violence. Consider the scenario in which you are at work while your entire family is enjoying a wonderful time in a unique atmosphere. There are only a few days in the year dedicated to those events. Is your employee's presence necessary? Well, if he or she is so indispensable, then you need to think twice before making him or her unhappy. As a manager, validate their holidays on special occasions without making your employees beg. As a CEO or HR director, ask around and include them on the company calendar (if not private, obviously). This way, everyone will know. Managers cannot justify a denial by ignorance, and employees can even wish their colleagues well. Of course, some projects may require their presence on an exceptional basis: but even then, recognise their sacrifice. Generally, people tend to be so devoted to their work that they are ready for sacrifice, as long as recognition is given (not necessary financially, although a bonus is always welcome).

Referring to the question posed in the preamble of this chapter, "Do you consider yourself as open?", I believe that our openness is still a work in progress. Depending on our background, education, values, and environment, we may be one step ahead or one step behind our peers. The key to the OPEN way is to continue to progress with patience...

Patience

Keep calm and discuss.

Patience is the quality of accepting and enduring changes, desired or not, with quietness.

Patience is probably one of today's most challenging attitudes. In a society where everything needs to go faster and better, the notion of pausing is counterintuitive. Yet we need it even more than before. Patience is twofold: patience towards others (commonly used) and towards ourselves. Depending on your personality, one may be much harder than the other one.

"It is almost like breaking yourself down to build yourself up again. Identifying the root causes of DEI and addressing them effectively takes a lot of time, effort, and the willingness to recognise mistakes."
Ilham Kadri

Irrational circle

The ego is a hindrance in this situation. As your ego grows, you will become less patient with your colleagues and your work. A sense of pride can lead to irrational reasoning and intense emotions that can cloud your judgment. Irrationality may lead you to act in a detrimental manner towards yourself and others. A vicious circle of failure sets in: the more you fail, the more impatient you become; the more impatient you become, the more failure you experience. This may negatively affect your sense of self-worth. The good news is that if you accept it, you can rebuild from it. If you think with impatience, that is the biggest failure. For example, if a project was not successfully accomplished, you may take it personally, which can impede any attempt to correct it. As a matter of fact, it is perfectly normal to fail, to sometimes feel "not good enough". Isabel admires some US companies who recognised their failure.

"George Floyd's death has created a whole movement in the States. For instance, Levi's and Nike acted on it and openly admitted that although their advertising might show a diverse brand, internally they are not diverse and inclusive enough. It is unfortunate that somebody had to be killed first, but what came out of this gives hope for the future."
Isabel Verstraete

Indeed, the Black Lives Matter Movement[19] has put pressure on U.S. and E.U. companies to report on racial diversity, while they have been reluctant to do so. In the E.U., large companies with over 500 employees must include data on the diversity of the board in the non-financial statement. In the U.S., FORTUNE[20] has gone further by announcing that they will *"make corporate diversity disclosure the new standard of doing business... FORTUNE will launch a new D&I filter that will allow companies on the 2021 FORTUNE 500 List to be sorted and ranked using a company's self-reported data, provided by Refinitiv[21]."* FORTUNE CEO Alan Murray says, *"What gets measured gets managed. Until companies commit to measuring and disclosing their diversity data, it will be hard to make progress."[22]* While Refinitiv CEO David Craig commented, *"By teaming up with FORTUNE to create Measure Up, har-*

nessing their unique link with the CEO community, I'm more hopeful than ever that the corporate world can fulfil its promises and respond to the cries for change that have only grown louder in the wake of the murder of George Floyd."

In 2020, Refinitiv launched a Diversity & Inclusion index; an analysis on D&I trends[23] was conducted using a universe of 3,722 firms with ESG scores for the years 2014–2018 compared to 2019. Amongst others, they found:
- 30% of board members are culturally diverse
- 43% increase in number of females on the board in the last five years
- 54% increase in the number of firms with official flexible working policies
- 25% increase in the number of firms with a career development policy.

Trends are therefore positive, including in terms of ways of working. Unfortunately, as in much research, the focus was on appearances, which is relevant, but not enough to measure diversity, equity, and inclusiveness in a firm.

Fighting the body

Sometimes the fight is with your body. One day, I realised that I could not wake up. My body was not following my orders; my brain had lost command. I was so tired, and let's admit it, psychologically depressed. Later, I understood I was at the limit of burnout. I was abroad, with no family or friends to take care of me. I had to take sick leave. I slept. I did not know what to do, so I took a paintbrush, and I started painting. I had bought the items some weeks ago and registered for a class, but never had the time to go. Correction: I never took the time to attend; allocation of priorities is the issue, not the availability of time. I spent hours painting. I felt a strong yearning for my piano – unfortunately it is not easy to take it with me when travelling. At one point, I felt exhausted again and went back to bed. The next day, I woke up hungry and realised that I had not eaten in the past 30 hours. After a decent breakfast, I went back to work. I was still fragile, so a week later, when people started screaming in a meeting, I left. I went walking in the streets in almost half a metre of snow, without a coat. I was not cold; on the contrary, I felt warm. After 30 minutes, I came back, and they were still shouting, I slapped the table, and demanded that they sit and listen. I scared myself and my manager. I had just said "Shut up and listen" to a French director – the kind of guy who thought it normal to be on first-name terms with me when I was supposed to be on last-name terms with him. I was not at all in control of what I was doing. In fact, I was not sure of what happened; I had to ask my colleagues to tell me. Apparently, I reminded them of the objective of the meeting and asked those not invited to leave (yes, some were not even invited). I drew a table with the outputs expected and insisted, "Nobody will leave this meeting until we agree on these points. Now, who wants to say something? Nobody? Then we are doing a round table."

My manager feared I would quit or get fired; he did not see any other options. Actually, that half-hour walk had saved me from both options and most importantly, from burnout. That was a critical moment of my career, when I realised that taking time out of work was important for work. Getting rid of destructive emotions to focus on the positive ones, that was within my control zone. I thought toxic feelings were imposed on me. They were not: I had let them get to me. I started going to some painting classes, no matter the professional urgency. I went to the gym at noon once a week, no matter the workload. I went jogging on a beautiful island, no matter how tired I felt and whatever the weather. With no natural social activities, I enforced my participation in three per week. Taking the time for non-productive activities was helping me be much more productive. I have worked better since then. During stressful times, I was a support to my colleagues who needed to express their emotions without absorbing them or amplifying them. Enjoying moments to yourself is a sustainable investment that helps you to gain more focus and be more human. In the short term, it can be seen as a waste of time, or the wrong allocation of priorities. Patience helps you to see the long-term impact.

Enjoying moments to yourself is a sustainable investment that helps you to gain more focus and be more human.

> **"** *Desires make slaves out of kings and patience makes kings out of slaves.* **"**
> **Abu Hamid Al-Ghazali**

Positively moving

Patience is also linked to positivity. By taking a step back, you can put things in perspective, and turn negativity into opportunity. Every leader knows the power of an objective in which everyone believes – mountains can be shifted. Thibaut Georgin believes in positivity as an enabler for inclusion.

> *"I take your experience: I think that you could change the way people are working and say, 'Let's collaborate because it's in your interest to collaborate.' For that, you also need to have empathy. Positive doesn't mean being naive but fixing objectives to be in a positive spirit spiral. It's something I'm trying to work on, because it is important to include all people on the boat."*
> **Thibaut Georgin**

"Even bad publicity is free publicity." As a marketeer, Isabel Verstraete feels that change will happen through talking about it, even if the intention is not (yet) there.

It is true that the more people talk about it, the more they get educated and ready to act, if the message is accurate enough. When I asked Satish Kumar about my worry that DEI is being used as a fashionable concept, he answered that the positive side of humanity is stronger than anything else. As a peace activist, who walked 13,000 km through 15 countries, from New Delhi to Moscow, Paris, London and Washington and then from Tokyo to Hiroshima, we can rely on his word.

"I walked through Muslim, Christian, Communist, Capitalist, rich, poor countries; I met black, white, brown, educated, illiterate people, peasants, business leaders and so on. I was welcomed by all people. I had no money yet for 2 ½ years I survived on the generosity and hospitality of strangers. There is a positive side to humanity; people are able to rise and transcend their prejudices and therefore in whatever way we can, we should promote the cause of diversity and inclusivity and not worry about the cause being fashionable or not."
Satish Kumar

Human beings are capable of wonderful and awful things. In a way, Satish's beautiful act is a direct consequence of war horrors. Doesn't this contradiction reflect the history of mankind?

" *You don't hire for skills; you hire for attitude. You can always teach skills.* "
Simon Sinek

Patience enables creativity. I realised that when I decided to work less. In fact, I was less in front of a computer, less in meetings, less in offices. But my mind kept working. Our brain is surprising. A bit like my mum: even without asking, she gives us guidance and opinions. For instance, writing those lines was a challenge. I needed to book some time alone, prioritise writing over operational duties, and face the syndrome of the blank page. One day I was so tired that I could not work. I felt guilty and stressed: my editor was waiting for some pages. I had given three trainings the days before, had been to various events; I had no energy left. So, I talked to myself, had a nice multi-way chat with the voices in my head, and decided to accept the usefulness of the day. I ate well, had a nap, played piano, watched TV enrobed in a blanket in the middle of the day. Then, as the sun was shining, I went for a walk in a park. Suddenly, my brain sent me ideas for the empty chapter: it came so fast that I needed to write them immediately in my phone notes. Back home, I started writing with passion and almost caught up with the plan (well, I was still late). If I had kept pushing and forcing my body to remain in front of the computer and commanded my hands to produce, I am pretty sure I would not have reached that level, even if I had dedicated the whole day. Our mind and body talk to us, not in words but in feelings and signs. We just need to open the way for listening patiently. As an example, I worked with Youssef, a colleague who is highly creative, but who was so last-minute that I was stressing out about his schedule. He sat in front of his computer the afternoon before an important presentation, watching a video on his phone while listening to the radio on the computer. "How do you focus?" I asked him. He looked at me puzzled. He did not know how, but the noise helped him to concentrate. As he explained to me, he was unable to start in advance, but I did not need to worry as he was constructing the slides for his presentation. As we worked together, I needed a lot of patience to accept that his way is fundamentally different from mine. His creativity was triggered in a completely different manner than mine.

Timely decisions

—

"I like the P of patience because when we try to be too quick, it can create frustration. Sometimes, people are not happy and want to push harder, but it can be counterproductive.

The first thing is: taking time to understand the context. A lot of differences are linked to a different perception. It's important that we, as a board, have the full information.

The second point is: what is our intention and what would we like to achieve? Taking that distance allows us to find a third way or a consensus with which everybody is happy. Happy doesn't mean crazy enthusiastic. At the end, I often ask the question "Can you live with that?" Probably there are people happier than others, but at least there are no frustrated persons. In fifteen years as board member and as chairman, I never reached a point where we had to vote."

Thibaut Georgin

—

In a board of directors, there are two trends: the ones who avoid too many discussions and decide by majority, and the others who argue until reaching a consensus. With the drive of my youth, I preferred majority votes. Let's act! Let's continue! Now, I tend to favour consensus (I got older). I like having everyone on board. Being on a board of a public institution where none chose the other and none knew the other before, I can tell you that reaching a consensus is challenging. "Sometimes it is better to just vote," a colleague said. There are times when it may be necessary, for instance, in the case of a major change. For day-to-day business decisions, the answer is generally no. It is true that through negotiations, you may feel that you lost your point. If you want to pass a bill to give 200 euros to people and end up with 100 euros, it may be seen as a lost cause. However, 100 euros agreed on by everyone (well technically, disagreed on by no one) is a sustainable action. The 200 euros agreed upon by five directors out of nine will be contested very quickly, and the situation can be reset to square one with 0 euros being allocated.

"I don't like to vote because it usually means the majority wins and the majority is not always right. It is also a consequence of who is more charismatic, not always because of better arguments. Some people might have the best ideas but as more introvert, they're not considered. I also try always to push for a consensus. It is more inclusive."
Hanan Challouki

"It depends on the type of environment: is it non-profit, is it for profit, is it private, is it public? There is no board structure applicable to all. Consensus is nice, but if everybody agrees to agree or abandons some tough battles, you may not be bold and precise, not enough to address some of the challenges. Inclusion in the board of directors needs to allow for diversity of thoughts and divergent thinking. We can have gender parity, different nationalities in the room, but if we think alike, it will go against good performance and prosperity. If consensus means only taking the common denominator, you are maybe missing the big elephant in the room, which is destroying value and harming the company."
Ilham Kadri

The decision process has a direct impact on team cohesion and on responsibility sharing. When someone votes against a decision that is contested afterwards, the person can easily declare, "I was against it. Look in the meeting minutes!" Clearly, that is not fair game. That is also why I am against minutes recording nominatively what each person has said. Whenever you are concerned about potential harm to the company, you fight for it and do more than simply express your opposition: you block the decision. There are many ways to block a decision, within and outside a meeting. If not, you should bear the consequences of the collective decision along with your colleagues. Perhaps the company would have been better off with your approach, or perhaps it would have been worse. It is impossible to guarantee that any decision will be the best one. Based on the current context, we believe that this is the right course of action we can take. Of course, it requires more time to reach a consensus: everyone will express their arguments, then solutions will be proposed, refused, some parts will be accepted by some and not by the others, words will circle around until finally, after an exhaustive period, a decision can be reached that everyone can live with. You might think: "Even like this, some people state that they are not responsible." Yes, they can say that, but in the end, the fact is that they accepted the proposal. Everyone is responsible. Consensuses are time consuming but much more sustainable than majority vote. After all, consensus etymology derives from the Latin word "consentire", meaning "feel together". A decision felt together.

Consensus is not unanimity. The first one is when no one disagrees; the second, when everyone agrees. The difference may seem subtle, yet it is fundamental. If you consider the diversity of thoughts, all your people agreeing on everything is almost impossible. When you are a board member, making decisions about every item can be very exhausting. Depending on the topic, you may wish to rely on your colleagues' expertise. You follow the discussion, of course, but do not see anything to add. The act of voting triggers a sudden wish for deep analysis and control, which can be very inefficient.

——

Diversity of members and openness in the debates are prerequisites for the effectiveness of any decision-making type.

——

Diversity of members and openness in the debates are prerequisites for the effectiveness of any decision-making type, even the one you believe to be the most efficient. Philippe Urfalino, a French sociologist, analysed cultural policies and the sociology of decision and deliberation. He concluded that even though consensus allows people to not make up their mind and to "decide without dividing", it is not an egalitarian form of collective decision-making, as it is based on a general acceptance of the unequal weight among participants.

"The general equality of participation in the process coexists with a prevailing recognition of the legitimacy of unequal influence of individuals, depending on social status or expertise... As a consequence, the democratic character of this rule of decision has to be weighted depending on whether we emphasise the equality of each with regard to participation in the debating process or the equal weight of each in the final result."[24].

Isabelle Ferreras is an expert on democracy in a company, seeing it as a way for workers to be a member of the organisation.

"Democratising the firm is the way forward to recognise workers as equal in dignity and rights, based on the recognition of their contribution. Each worker should have a say on the collective endeavour that is the firm or the organisation, through an equivalent of the shareholders General Assembly, what I call a "labour investors' general assembly". It should elect its workers' representatives, and that council should meet as regularly as the board. In Belgium, we already have such a council – it's the works council, which should be truly considered as a second legislative chamber for the firm."
Isabelle Ferreras

Our bicameral[25] political framework (i.e., having two separate elected assemblies: the House of Representatives and the Senate) could be applied inside an organisation.

"Through economic bicameralism, we ensure that those who are governed by the decisions of the firm are capable of consent to these decisions".
Isabelle Ferreras

Then, if one agrees with this radically different model, the representation must be inclusive, which is an issue today.

"Work councils should be exemplary in seeking to represent the diversity of the firm's workforce. Let's take the cleaning industry for instance. The workforce is heavily female with a minority background, yet you will see more often than not male representatives elected by the workforce.

My hope is that as we move forward with the quest of democratising the firm, more and more we will bring this conversation about equal inclusion and equal representation.

It will not happen just because we make a structural change, because we grant workers the ability to validate or veto the decisions of the board. It is to be leveraged with an intention to make inclusion a central part of this democratic agenda."
Isabelle Ferreras

Mondragon operates today according to this model of democracy, with around 80,000 workers. It is a corporation and federation of worker cooperatives based in the Basque region of Spain, selling in more than 150 countries. The industrial cooperative was established in 1955 by a priest, José María Arizmendiarrieta, and five of his students. With the credo "humanity at work", they describe themselves as "an entrepreneurial socio-economic project inspired by the principles of our cooperative experience:
- Democracy: 1 partner 1 vote,
- Solidarity: pay scale 1 to 6,
- Participation: ownership, management, and results,
- Intercooperation: shared funds / relocations.

A project created by and for people in line with fairness, self-imposed standards, and co-responsibility."[26] With more than 50 years' experience and yearly revenues of around 11 billion euros, the case is used to demonstrate alternative ownership and management systems, although they have their challenges to keep their principles while operating worldwide.

Thierry Geerts believes that inclusion facilitates better decision-making, even though he does not believe a company can be a democracy.

"A company cannot be full democracy. Somebody needs at certain moments to make tough choices. The risk is that people do not dare and make dangerous fluffy decisions. Do a round table to be sure that the more introverted are also talking; look at body language. Sometimes one person is right, and all the others are wrong. The decision's quality is far better because more voices are heard."
Thierry Geerts

Francis Blake too, believes that it is the CEO and the top of the organisation who decides in the end, while ensuring inclusive listening. However, in board meetings, he is also prone to consensus.

"In my 25 years' experience as a board member, I have only experienced one out of the hundreds of decisions, where we had to vote. The rest is always consensus because members have a personal responsibility and are responsible for their own money. If they don't agree with the decision taken, they will resign. There are compromises, with a lot of politics on the side. If you believe that your idea is not going to pass, you know who you are going to see before the meeting."
Francis Blake

Decisions made by a manager and his or her team and those made by a board of directors do not follow the same process. I asked Harold Boël, an experienced leader managing a global investment holding, Sofina. He has worked extensively on governance solutions. His argument draws upon the notion of personal responsibility presented by Francis Blake, completing it by pointing out the asymmetry of information between these two positions. As stated in the introduction, information is power.

"In a management team, the level of information is spread roughly equally among participants, each contributing his or her take on the subject. Diversity is a source of added value as a kaleidoscope of viewpoints is brought to the table. Voting makes little sense, as the manager carries the responsibility.

On a board of directors, the chair is 'only' a decision's midwife. Board's workings are dialogues between management and directors in which there is an asymmetry of information between board members, only knowing the information shared, and management, having access to all the information. Board diversity favours a shared holistic view on the context, a sensitivity difficult to acquire by management alone. Consensus is important because the board carries collegial responsibility. Voting is the sign of the inability to form a common view. No single viewpoint carries truth, so, ideally, decisions need to encompass all of them, without diluting the quality of the decision to the lowest common denominator. It's an alchemy and a balance that successful boards learn to achieve."

Harold Boël

In one context, consensus makes sense; in another, it does not. Being in the same organisation does not determine one way of collaborating. In any case, impatience cannot be the main driver.

The idea that clear role allocation enables full inclusion seduced me. I wondered whether the structure of an organisation has a direct impact on inclusion. I have worked in a classical hierarchical department which was transformed into holacracy. The decision-making process is straightforward: you decide your role, then people can object, but only if it impacts their role. I was tired of long and inefficient meetings where everyone has a say in everything, so at first, I liked it. Until I saw some very stupid decisions in which I was not allowed to intervene and provide warnings, strictly following the rule. Despite my attempts, the facilitator repeatedly said, "This is not a valid objection." Says who? The holacracy bible. That is when I disconnected from those principles. Collective intelligence exists in every organisation, which is why it would be a shame not to use it. Holacracy has many good principles, but something essential was missing in our change management: the mind needs to be open and people need to be listening with patience. Answering: "It's like this because it's the rule; it's written here, look," is very alienating. We are not robots. We are human beings with a super brain pushing us to constantly innovate. So, if you are interested in holacracy, please adapt the rules when they do not fit. Replacing a bible with another one without a change in mentality will not be of any help. As an example, I kept a lesson learnt from holacracy: starting every meeting with a check-in. The meeting begins with a round table discussion in which everyone expresses their feelings. It's not about giving personal details, but about simply expressing how you feel. A colleague who informs you that he did not sleep well because his child is teething is likely to be distracted and irritable. A colleague who tells you she got good news just before entering the room will be enthusiastic (not necessarily because of the meeting content). This increases the efficiency of meetings while adding a human touch to daily work.

Educating stereotypes

Fighting unconscious bias requires a lot of patience. A lot is determined in our education. With the Ras El Hanout non-profit organisation, we were creating a theatre piece based on the civil right movements and travelling to get as much information and inspiration as we could. I discovered a powerful study during a trip in the United States, back in the dark days of racial segregation. The Clark's doll experiment[27] was performed in 1940: children were presented with two identical dolls, with only skin and hair colour variation. One female doll was white with blonde hair, the other was brown with black hair. The children were asked which one they preferred, and a large preference was for the white doll. The conclusions exposed internalised racism and self-hatred from children in African-American schools. The illustration of those damaging effects helped show that the statement "separate but equal" was false, and therefore facilitated the end of segregation in schools. This study was performed several times after racial segregation was legally abolished in 1964, and the results were similar, indicating that unconscious bias still exists[28].

In some schools, education has evolved to deconstruct stereotypes, like in Isabel Verstraete's daughter's school.

"A fascinating experiment was given to my daughter at school, when she was twelve years old. They showed a picture of a man and a woman dressed in white doctors' uniforms, and they asked, "Who is the nurse and who is the doctor?" The whole class replied, "The woman is the nurse, and the man is the doctor." We instinctively have learnt to place our opinion based on appearance. This aspect is related to identity covering in the workplace, when employees deliberately hide something about themselves to avoid uncomfortable interactions."
Isabel Verstraete

Identity covering is where the "normal" is created and the "non normal" to be "integrated" is developed.

"Inclusion is when I see a person with disability, black men, or women wearing the veil working and people feeling at ease because it is just in the company culture. I am pleased that the person is there because of his or her skills and not to fill a quota."
Ibrahim Ouassari

So many times, I found myself in situations where I felt hurt, but could not react impulsively. Like at a dinner, where a friend was telling her mother, "This is Ihsane; she just graduated from Solvay magna cum laude." The mother kept staring at Marie, a blonde girl, who obviously was not named Ihsane. But still, for that woman, it was so impossible that someone *like me* graduated from Solvay with a high score. It had to be the other person sitting next to me. Even though the friend continued to insist, "No Mom, not Marie, I am talking about Ihsane, sitting next to her." What could I do? Cry? Shout, "Do you have a problem understanding that I graduated, me, not her?" I smiled. I let others think I was not hurt; it was just a small misunderstanding.

A short time ago, I was invited to participate in an event as a speaker. When I arrived, I stood in a line to register. The receptionist asked me my name. As usual, I had to spell it, "Ihsane, not Ishane. The h before the s, otherwise the sound is "ch". Haouach starting with an H." When she searched through her list, she did not find my name. "Are you sure you registered?" "Yes ma'am." The situation was deemed suspicious by her colleague, who stepped in to assist her. "Ma'am, if you are not in the list, then you cannot enter. Please leave the building." Upon my insistence, she began to stress as if she was the one responsible for the nuclear code and that I was attempting to steal it. The colour of her face became red, her body was sweating, and her eyes were searching desperately for the security guard, while watching my every movement (my Mediterranean heritage made it difficult for her to follow my gestures). One of the organisers passed by and hugged me. "Oh Ihsane, so great to see you. We were waiting for you; I stepped out of the auditorium to call you." Both receptionists appeared disconcerted. A smile spread across my face, and I said, "I told you I was on the list." One understood: "Oh you are a speaker! Why didn't you say so?" I censured myself because my answer would have been: "I was unaware that there were several lists, which is your responsibility. The question was not asked, since it seemed impossible to you that a person looking like me could be a speaker."

Hanan Challouki and Audrey Hanard have encountered many situations where their appearance was not considered as matching their role, not only because of their gender. When multiple classes of disadvantages are experienced by people because of their different social identities, we talk about intersectionality. Although the concept existed, the term was coined by Kimberlé Crenshaw[29] in 1989, who stated, "*Intersectionality is a metaphor for understanding the ways that multiple forms of inequality or disadvantage sometimes compound themselves and create obstacles that often are not understood among conventional ways of thinking.*"[30]   All of us are members of simultaneous interconnected social categories. For instance, Audrey Hanard has perceived different treatment not only because she was a woman, but also because she was young. A young man would not have the same experience; neither would an older woman. Hanan Challouki suffered inequality not only because she is a woman, or young, or a Muslim, or of a foreign background: it's because of all of that.

"In some instances, people would treat me differently: they addressed me using the familiar form ('tu') while they were using a more formal form ('vous') for others at the same hierarchical level, which is probably built based on age and gender; it's interesting because it generates a different power dynamic. And it can actually go both ways: I've experienced older men talking formally to me while talking familiarly to my male colleagues because they were uncomfortable being too close to a woman. However, both lead to the exact same feeling: I felt like others were included, and I was treated separately.

It has happened a few times that clients would look at male consultants of my team, rather than looking at me. Even if they knew I was the manager, somehow it was difficult for them to click."
Audrey Hanard

"I would go to a meeting with one of my colleagues, a white, blonde woman. People would always assume that she was my employer. They would start talking to her and not realise that I am the strategist. That's how you feel bias in conversations and bias that leads to certain decisions."
Hanan Challouki

If you encounter such a situation once, it is manageable. But when it becomes routine, it is harder. Then you elaborate strategies. For me, humour has always been one of the best ways to react. Denial can help as well. Like in meetings, when you realise that some tasks are strangely systematically allocated to you, the only woman, the youngest, the only one of foreign origin. "Sorry, I cannot serve you coffee, I am so clumsy." "I really cannot take notes; my writing is worse than a doctor's." I know they were not aware of it. Sometimes, saying it directly does not help. Repeated straightforward discussions about DEI are not helpful. You can be directly catalogued as "the feminist", you know those "hysterical women who see harm in everything".

"Some senior colleagues would never invite young women for lunch (in practice, informal mentoring and coaching sessions) because they felt uncomfortable. It was not ill-intended, purely because they were afraid of how it would be perceived (trying to seduce or flirt with younger women). Therefore, young female professionals did not always have access to the same level of informal support as their male peers."
Audrey Hanard

Once, I was working from my previous company's Parisian offices. My colleague, Beatrice, went to print some documents. She came back with a bunch of papers and asked me, "Are you going to see Patrick in your next meeting? His assistant asked me to print those for him. Could you please give them to him?" I took the folder and was happily going to do the small favour. Then, something struck me. I asked her, "Do you often print documents for him?" She answered: "Yes, apparently he does not know how to print in Paris, so if his assistant did not receive the documents in advance to prepare them for him, she always asks me." I was shocked. Beatrice was a director, at the same hierarchical level as Patrick. They were in the same board meeting, had the same type of heavy responsibilities. Beatrice also had an assistant to prepare her documents. Despite this, the secretary (a woman) relied on the only woman on the board to print the man's papers since she perceived that either the task was beneath him, or he was not capable of doing it himself (or both). Oh, those unconscious biases are so strong!

I advised Beatrice to express her concern to the assistant, which she did. She also went to Patrick's computer and installed the printer for him. Let's specify that here the man had no problem doing his last-minute printing himself. Of course, he could have noticed the bizarre situation, but he did not act wrongly. Sexist behaviour is not only male-based: it is a human unconscious phenomenon embedded in our society. Like racism, thoughts can be carried by people of colour themselves. Some stereotypes are so structurally embedded in our society that it is hard to first recognise them, then get rid of them. Therefore, regular training needs to be organised. Prepare your employees for cultural diversity, unconscious bias, conflict resolution, interpersonal communication... and don't forget patience and empathy! Educate your organisation's members about the differences between inclusion, inclusivity, diversity, and ... discrimination, whether it is positive or negative. Do not be afraid of the word. Despite being less glamorous than diversity, discrimination is a reality.

—

Sexist behaviour is not only male-based: it is a human unconscious phenomenon embedded in our society.

—

Excluding by talking

Language is an attention point, specifically in organisations with international scope – or simply established in Brussels.

One day, I was chatting with Jonathan, a colleague, in the coffee corner. Kevin, another colleague, came over to us. He was British; he spoke neither French nor Dutch. He tried to express a frustration. His cheeks were red, he was playing with the carpet with his feet, and his tone was low. He mumbled: "Ihsane, Jonathan, I know that you don't do it on purpose, but would it be possible, please, to speak English, please, just so I can participate... if it is okay for you?" Jonathan promptly responded, "Don't worry, if we need to speak to you, we will do it in English." In his sincere response, he was inconsiderate. In his mind, there was no issue: a practical question was asked, and it was answered. My friend Harold, who manages an international organisation, described the same experience to me, where the answer was, "But we are on a break and talking about our weekend." The social dynamics can be such a violent experience for the individuals attempting to be included! Having a conversation about anything makes a team cohesive. There is no malice involved here; most people are unaware of their comments' effects. Therefore, they need to be educated on this issue.

If you do not talk the language, you cannot participate, so you are excluded. I also noticed a difference in lunch period: most Flemish people ate around noon, while most French-speaking persons, around one o'clock. Is it cultural or just specific to that department? I do not know, but it is so sad to have such a barrier. It is however understandable that at lunch time, people just want to speak their native language. A leader must address the needs of these communities in a manner that promotes cohesion while considering individual specificities.

In Belgium, where three official languages are spoken (Dutch, French, German) as well as a multitude of non-official languages and dialects, this poses a significant challenge. As with any challenge, it can either be an asset or a liability.

According to Thierry Geerts, Belgium's diversity and its language complexity offer a tremendous opportunity. Similarly, Ilham Kadri shares that through her extensive international experience, she was charmed by the diversity that can be found in Belgium and Brussels.

"Diversity is definitely an asset for Belgium. Brussels is one of the most diverse democratic cities in the world[31]! That is why Brussels is so amazing. It's not one community; it is all! Whatever you imagine on diversity; you have in Brussels. Being bilingual is a super asset. We have a government with a lot of parties because we have diverse opinions in Belgium. We combine that plurality with democracy, which is not an obvious thing."

 Thierry Geerts

"I travelled in many countries with my family. Of course, we need to improve, but in general, Belgium is a welcoming country. Brussels is extremely cosmopolitan in terms of the number of foreigners per capita, for example. We have the European Union and the North Atlantic Treaty Organization, which bring diversity of nationalities and more. Brussels has very good schools, therefore foreigners can bring their families along, and as an employer, this is important. Brussels' inclusive environment is refreshing, yet underrepresentation remains. We don't have enough minorities represented in our corporations, especially at the top level."

Ilham Kadri

" *Great things are done by a series of small things brought together.* **"** **Vincent Van Gogh**

Incremental trend

DEI cannot be viewed as a fashion trend. People's lives are affected by it. The common goal should therefore be kept in mind when developing a strategy. If you are motivated and convinced, you may feel compelled to act immediately and feel that your current actions are not sufficient. Incremental changes will undoubtedly take time, but transformative changes (more radical) may not be sustainable. There is a possibility that you may have to go back to square one and take more time than if you advanced gradually with small steps. In order to determine when to push and when to slow down, one must feel the momentum. The process of change requires patience. A Gartner study[32] demonstrates that just 34% of all change initiatives pursued by businesses end in clear success, and a further 16% yield mixed results. This equates to 50% of all change initiatives failing. Harvard

Business Review[33] sees three main reasons: poor employee buy-in, a lack of clear vision, inadequate understanding among managers.

Depending on where you start, the efforts will be different. Francis Blake points out the difference in size and history for each organisation.

"Some organisations, specially managed by younger people, are more interested in developing diversity and inclusion because they realise that this is the best way to ensure a better future for all. It is more difficult for larger organisations with history to include diversity in all the processes, as diversity was just something that they mentioned in their yearly report."
Francis Blake

Change is most necessary for those who do not possess the power to effect it easily. The power holders, on the other hand, do not perceive the need for change: that is why they require an incentive. The current vagueness of inclusion has caused many white men to feel threatened. Their world is shrinking as it is growing for people who have different looks and appearances. Some men are refused employment because of their gender. They are right; it is difficult. I am aware of this because I have also been denied opportunities due to my background. The difference is that it was not always said straight out, hence less contestable. Verna Myers, a world-known inclusion strategist, has developed training on the "evolving role of white men in the workplace". She encourages people to "talk boldly".

Change is most necessary for those who do not possess the power to effect it easily.

" *Talk boldly isn't about talking defiantly; it's about talking courageously and compassionately... Many men, and white men in particular, tell me they feel uncomfortable, excluded and worried about their professional careers in today's workplace... I get it. In many ways the workplace has changed, and it will continue to change as we make our organisations fairer and more inclusive of those who have been historically excluded and marginalised. But I believe that ultimately all of us will benefit from these efforts.* **"**
Verna Myers[34]

Verna Myers is the author of the famous quote: *"Diversity is being invited to the party. Inclusion is being asked to dance."* Fatima Zibouh[35], a Brussels social entrepreneur, completes it by an appeal to radical inclusion, which is not only being invited to dance, but also participating in *"organising the party"* to *"pay attention to everybody"*. Then, it takes a first candidate.

The first one to participate has a tricky role: the *first* woman to get that position, the *first* person of colour to reach that level, the *youngest* person to have that title, the first with a *handicap* to ever accomplish this... The first person with a visible difference from the "others", the "normal", breaks the ice-ceiling (generally, not without getting small pieces of glass in the skin). I have been often considered as the "first". One young woman trained in my non-profit organisation once wrote, "Thank you, Ihsane. I stopped counting the number of times you were the first to open doors for all of us." It has its significance. But was it the first time for someone with my personality type? Probably not. It is all about symbols. It is harder to track a difference with the type of personality. Hanan Challouki knows it too well. I asked her about how she felt when she was in a non-diverse assembly:

"Lonely, like you are far from everybody else. It is not a pleasant experience. For example, at an event, I was literally the only person of colour in a room with four hundred marketeers. I thought, 'This room shows that there's something very wrong in our industry.' They are all nice people, but how can they not see that? I texted my husband and I told him: 'I don't feel good. I wish you had come with me.' He told me: 'Next year will be better.' That is how we move forward, how we try to make a difference. We normalise things so that hopefully in the upcoming years, there will be more."

Hanan Challouki

Her words could have been mine. Indeed, I feel lonely at first, then, I talk to people and realise I am not that different. The only barrier remaining is when people stare at us thinking we are animals in a zoo: to be analysed, or even touched. I am not kidding, it happened that a lady wanted to touch my head, to see what it felt like. You can imagine my reaction: I was not in a mood to address her with humour. Most of the time, the ice melts and fun takes over. Patience helps me to bring positivity and generosity to an event.

" *Talent is long patience.* "   **Gustave Flaubert**

Remembering the known

I constructed training on talents – how to identify and develop talents, especially in change management. One thing I insist on: if work needs patience, patience needs work. It takes patience to develop patience. It is a way not only to improve our individual and collective performance but also to reach a happier life. We all know theories about how we need to be less stressed, particularly with our kids. But the school rhythm is stressful, let alone professional life. I often criticise myself, for instance, when I tell my daughter to "Hurry up" in the morning. I tell myself, "You know you can't say this; you will stress her and because of you, she will become a tense adult." I correct to "It's okay, take your time." Then, "Just keep the pace, please." Well, we have no choice, in ten minutes she needs to be at school and in thirty minutes I need to be at work. With moral reminders, we can improve ourselves step by step. I don't think that because of a nice theory of happiness we can change all our habits, but we can slowly advance. Just taking a deep breath in a moment of tension releases a lot of stress. A time investment of ten seconds can be highly profitable. If I don't do it, how can I expect others to do it? Leading by example is necessary for any change. Your commitment must be inspiring so that others engage.

A mentality switch is already happening. According to the World Happiness Report 2022, wellbeing is linked to notions of equity and sustainability.

The use of the word "happiness" is growing as much as the use of the word "income" is decreasing. The word wellbeing, in its various forms, is increasing in popularity and is more often being used to connote sustainability and equality, in addition to its older range of meanings... the role and prominence of happiness and its related concepts and terminology are on the rise... In the last quarter century, the words "happiness" and "income" have undergone opposite trajectories, respectively doubling and halving their use in printed books.[36]

The good news is: as diversity brings more happiness, this positive emotion results in more performance. McKinsey's latest study[37] concluded that implementation of DEI is profitable, while lack of it is penalising. However, the analysis points out the slow improvement in terms of representation.

...there is a substantial performance differential – 48% – between the most and least genderdiverse companies.

The business case for inclusion and diversity is stronger than ever. For diverse companies, the likelihood of outperforming industry peers on profitability has increased over time, while the penalties are getting steeper for those lacking diversity.

Progress on representation has been slow, yet a few firms are making real strides. A close look at these diversity winners shows that a systematic, business-led approach and bold, concerted action on inclusion are needed to make progress.

Though patience is required, certain acts should be treated with zero tolerance: microaggressions. These can be expressed as direct attacks or as jokes that are presented as harmless. Humour is a very powerful tool to marginalise certain opinions. If you repeat enough sayings about Roma stealing, people will believe that this is reality. A few years ago, we got robbed. When the police arrived, I showed them all the relevant indices I had compiled. They stopped me: "Ma'am, we are not on a TV show." Then, one of them asserted: "This is the work of Romani people. We heard some were living in the neighbourhood." I told them: "How can you say that, if there is no proof?" He replied: "Because this is their style. The robbery was not planned; they just came and did not even see that there was an alarm. They took what they could in two minutes and left a mess. I know my work, Ma'am." It shocked me: this was a policeman making a racist remark as if it was a normal occurrence. I became angry and replied, "I am not sure which of your statements is the most frustrating: that Roma are thieves or that they are stupid thieves. Because if they were, at least they would have been smart and prepared for the crime. In your capacity as a representative of the state, are you aware that, without any proof, you are perpetuating racist perceptions? If I just believe you without thinking, I will say to all my friends, 'I was robbed by Romani people' while there is no evidence to prove who did it." His eyes were wide as he pondered my response. His colleague intervened by saying: "At least we did not say they were Arabs." The first police officer replied, "No, this is not the style of Arabs. They are a bit smarter." I was speechless. Their mindsets had been ingrained and ingrained for so many years that I failed to convince them with my arguments.

In the absence of early intervention, microaggressions can lead to harassment. In most cases, harassment is not obvious, particularly when it is committed by several people at the same time. One feeds the other until eventually no one recognises when the red line has been crossed. Collective irresponsibility results in a downward spiral of consequences. Individuals may not intend harm: they may believe that stereotypes are accurate. The problem will usually need to be detected by an external party. In this case as well, training is crucial to identify and address macroaggressions.

I was working with a colleague, Tim, who was homosexual. He was living in a small town in Flanders and did not meet many people of colour. His fear of me was evident when he joined the team. He was pleasant, polite, but he avoided me. While I respected that, I tried to approach him from time to time to let him know that I was not an enemy. A senior colleague used to come and bully him. Tim laughed at his homophobic jokes. I did not. Once, I asked him, "Are you not bothered by his jokes?" He hesitated a few seconds before answering, "I hate them. But what can I do? Getting angry will make me look like the crazy gay who can't handle a simple joke." He felt the company culture would not secure his right to be respected. But who defines the culture if not the people within it? A satisfactory answer is drawn by Pierre Gurdjian.

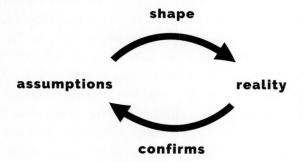

"The culture of an organisation can be defined as its collective per-sonality. That is neither static nor generic. It is a process, a gradual emergence shaped by people, events, and performance. It is often an unconscious process, particularly at collective level. It consists of for-mal elements like official values and narratives, but, more importantly, of the unstructured confluence of countless individual and team experi-ences and stories that get passed on from generation to generation. It is a continuous, organic bottom-up process defined by the daily realities and experiences of a multitude of concrete people of flesh and blood, living their lives as well as they can."

Pierre Gurdjian

The habits and values that we develop as employees, leaders, directors, managers, and members of an organisation are passed on to future generations. We have a greater responsibility than we realise. Each member shares an individual respon-sibility in the collective organisation.

" *One's philosophy is not best expressed in words; it is expressed in the choices one makes. In the long run, we shape our lives, and we shape ourselves. The process never ends until we die. And the choices we make are ultimately our own responsibility.* "
Eleanor Roosevelt

Do not undermine your own power. If nobody acts, who will?
As you develop qualities of openness and patience, you will be able to place your-self in others' shoes and grow empathy...

Empathy

Put yourself in their shoes.

Empathy is the ability to sense other people's emotions and connect to their thoughts, experiences, and feelings.

I discovered empathy when playing theatre. A friend once asked me, "Why do you need to spend all your weekends rehearsing for the play? You know your lines, that's it, right?" Performing is so much more than memorising a few lines. As a performer, you should embody the character, feel as she or he feels, and react in the same way that she or he does. Your mind, your heart and your body do not belong to you any more: you put them aside to embrace those of your character. The role is not on a script any more, you bring it to life. As a spectator, intensity and focus are necessary to watch a play, so that the feelings of the roles transcend you. Essentially, a lack of feeling means that either you were not concentrating, the play was not good, or the subject matter did not interest you. In general, culture serves as an excellent tool for addressing society's challenges. Wasn't Belgian independence triggered by an opera play: "The Mute Girl of Portici"[38]?

> **"** *I have learned silence from the talkative, tolerance from the intolerant, and kindness from the unkind; yet strangely, I am ungrateful to these teachers.* **"** **Khalil Gibran**

Every person lives different experiences. To gain knowledge about a situation, you must first experience it. You cannot comprehend what you have not encountered. You may be able to gain some understanding, sufficient to be able to help others who are struggling, even if you are not aware of what it is to experience it. Empathy is the best you can do to get close to someone else's emotions. We all have a different story linked to diversity and inclusion. Hanan Challouki, like me, was born of immigrant parents. In other words, we were literally immersed in these topics since our birth. Of course, it became more difficult when we decided to wear the headscarf. Inclusion became for us a "personal mission".

> *"I am a person from an ethnic minority in a country that is not always very open. I am part of a religious minority, I am a visible practising Muslim woman, and many people see images and prejudices, which prevent me from getting certain opportunities. I've been excluded in many ways. I have a son and I hope that he does not have to experience all the racism I felt in school. Even though I know the chances are very small that I can prevent it, at least I can do something within organisations to hopefully make it better."*
> **Hanan Challouki**

For other people, DEI arrive without notice and change their life tremendously. For Francis Blake, it came with the birth of his daughter.

"Diversity has been an integral part of my family life mainly since our third child was born, 32 years ago, with a physical handicap. People looked at her/us differently. We had to start living in a different way. It opened a new world for us. We felt alone with our challenge: none of our friends had such an experience. That has had a big impact for me on accepting different people."
Francis Blake

His wife, Dominique, radically changed her life: she quit her job to be dedicated to the inclusion of her daughter, Emily, in society. The fact that Emily was born into a "privileged family" opened a new world also for other children with similar conditions but with less influential parents. In a way, her disability was an enabler for those kids. Dominique and Francis created many projects in an area where there were not a lot of initiatives for kids like Emily. Now, she lives in semi-independence in an energy-passive house in the centre of Louvain-la-Neuve, called "Côte à Côte[39]", created by her parents and their friends. They wanted their daughter to live as "normally" as possible, without stereotypes. They emphasised the importance of her contribution to the local communities: disabled people tend to bring joy. Physical disabilities can also surprise us during our life. Patrick Demoucelle was partner and vice-president of Bain & Company, a world leader in strategy consulting, for over 10 years. He saw his life tremendously transformed when Parkinson's disease took control of his body.

> **❝** *I might not have much time left... That is why I am embarking on this new chapter of my life. Leaving a successful business career to follow my calling... Today marks a new chapter in the story of my life. It is a story of fear. And it is a story of hope. But let me leave you with this thought: whenever there is a story of fear and hope, there is a heart that is beating.* **❞**
> **Patrick Demoucelle**

His wife, Anne-Marie, also changed her path to support her husband's cause. Together, they created the "Demoucelle Parkinson Charity" nonprofit organisation[40]. As with the previous example, the fact that a person with resources (in terms of skills, money and network) has been diagnosed with a disease improves the chances for many less fortunate people to be cured.

For other persons, it is still a learning process, as for Isabel Verstraete. She admitted that her sensibility to DEI is quite recent and that she had worked in non-diverse environments for a long time.

 "My two daughters' friends are from different backgrounds, social classes, skin colour: that was a first encounter with a different world. Because I grew up in a completely white school in a small town. At birthday parties, you start to cater for kids who say: 'I eat halal', or 'I eat kosher' or 'I am a vegan'."
Isabel Verstraete

Some were sensitised the hard way. Thibaut Georgin was two years old when his father was beaten to death by extreme right activists from Vlaamse Militanten Orde (VMO) in 1970[41]. Afraid of being perceived as a victim, he avoids discussing it. He is nevertheless a victim. Victims are not to be shamed. We tend to dislike this status because it triggers pity and makes us feel weak, which harms our self-esteem and pride. As for myself, I had difficulty recognising and using the word. Until recently, I advised a woman who was sexually abused to embrace her status as a victim, because she needed to acknowledge the trauma. Instead of making her weak, this makes her strong because she faces it with courage. However, I realised that I had been giving advice I didn't follow myself (which is often the case, isn't it?).

"With time and the recent commemoration of the 50th anniversary of my father's death, I realised that it had shaped me. That event could have had different consequences, for instance, to be vengeful towards the Flemish people. It was never the case. I was always interested in learning about Flemish topics, to talk to them and to learn the language. It's so great to have those cultures in one country; it creates positive attitudes. It is like you had. I had the same discussion with Kenza Isnasni[42]. Something quite horrible and violent happens and still the effect is: let's not forget, let's use that to show the importance to collaborate with all our differences."

Thibaut Georgin

There are times when violence leads to more violence. There are times when it brings peace. Hopefully, Thibaut, Kenza, and many other victims of hate crimes did not fall into the vicious circle of hatred and instead focused on what binds us together: our humanity.

In 2021, I was appointed Government Commissioner on behalf of the Federal Secretary of State for the Institute for Gender Equality. This nomination caused me to experience one of the most difficult moments of my life. This was a short-lived venture: after enduring six weeks of intensive cyber-harassment, I resigned, not without learning from it. Some people did not like to see "a woman like me" in such a position, for various reasons. As the debate on the neutrality of the state and the wearing of ostentatious signs raged on, I was thrust into the media-political spotlight and instrumentalised from all sides. Dozens of articles appeared displaying my face, my name, without me asking for this attention. The "Ihsane Haouach affair" is a case that bears my name but is so far beyond me. Thousands of tweets and comments on social networks talked about me, without really talking about me. For weeks, the hashtag #ihsanehaouach was ranked among the top ten hashtags in Belgium. Around me, the fight was personified. I was stripped of my personality to become a symbol at the heart of a controversy. Beyond the political debates that should normally happen peacefully in a democracy, I suffered a campaign of cyberstalking from which I struggled to recover (I am probably still in the process of recovering). These were the most intense weeks of my life, and yet…

During the reconstruction process, my first instinct was to confront the perpetrators. It quickly became apparent that this would be a fruitless exercise: every word in such an atmosphere generates more words. Aggression can become a vicious cycle. I had to give up any hope of justice. I decided to take time for myself, to slow down my intensive career path. I realised that I was focused on producing: time to think and to create became rare. I was running and no longer knew why. So, I dared to stop. I felt the need to write, to tell what I had experienced, to raise awareness so that this would not happen to others. I was contacted by many women who gave me their support and told me about their alarming experiences with cyberbullying. I met new people, far from my networks. I felt the need for a change of scene. I also consulted. Not a psychologist, but experts in communication, strategy, and writing. They told me that I had "an incredible opportunity", "fantastic capital", that this experience could be a springboard for my future projects. I have never felt that way, even today. I tried to move on. My writing project appeared to be a salvation. Strictly speaking, I didn't want to write my own story; I wanted to raise the debate beyond my person. I try to bring my perspective on multiculturalism and to convey a message that's perhaps more audible. Thibaut Georgin's comment helped me to understand that, hopefully, I would not go unto hate either.

Collective persona

I reflected about change management projects and how a company culture is constructed. I asked myself: if we all have our individuality, would the sum of those individualities create humanity? Pierre Gurdjian had thought about it.

"If the culture of an organisation is defined as its collective personality, and that such a collective personality is the result of the continuous bottom-up process of weaving together individual personalities, then changing a collective persona requires changing individual life journeys.

I consciously use 'life journeys' rather than 'professional journeys' because I deeply believe that we cannot lead separate lives; we are one. So, the process of cultural change requires an extraordinary deep attention to individual change journeys."
Pierre Gurdjian

In other words, changing a company culture would be like changing one's ways: the difficult part would be changing one's habits. The fact that an individual has multiple identities must be embraced, as those identities constitute the company culture. I asked Pierre: if a company is one collective persona, what about society as a whole? Pierre completes his thought by seeing a parallel between the emergence of a collective personality at company and society levels.

"What is true for an individual organisation is also true for society as a whole... within an even more complex and subtle canvas of diversity. And here as well, it eventually centres on Being and Receiving. Being aware and accepting the inner diversity of any local/regional/national culture and developing the curiosity for the many ways different cultures and their own nuances can enrich and stimulate, rather than threaten."
Pierre Gurdjian

If diversity is a part of being, then empathy is even more needed to be and feel the other human being. As a collective of unique individuals, we create a unique organisation, a unique society, a unique humanity, which is constantly evolving.

" *Don't do unto others what you don't want done unto you.* " **Confucius**

Love is...

I have used this quote from Confucius as a mantra since I was a teenager. I avoid saying it because it could be construed as a Miss Belgium-like response. However, corporate culture is increasingly accepting talks about love, benevolence, and kindness. I was amazed to hear Francis Blake, a CEO, chairman, founder, talking about love in an organisation, and stating that love for oneself induces love for the other.

"More and more people are talking about love with a Big L within an organisation. That means that you accept the other person, you wish him or her the best and you do everything so that he or she feels the best way possible."
Francis Blake

So, Big Love it is. Have you experienced it? I have. Not in social activities, as one might think, but in the corporate world, in a big multinational capitalistic company. Rather, I experienced more low blows in the social sector than in the private sector. The lack of resources creates a highly stressful environment, which is exacerbated by the notion that poor performance is acceptable if it is done for a good cause. "The end justifies the means.[43]" There is no truth in that for me. The means needs to satisfy the why. To get the why of your organisation, you need to find your personal one. Leadership skills are not only for the CEO and directors, they are for everybody. I strongly believe in the power of training. Train your people on soft skills, not only hard skills. The latter are easier to develop. That is something missing in the Belgian education system today: we need to develop soft skills starting at school. For instance, book conflict resolution training for your management team, then for the rest of the organisation. Do not complain about not having a budget; one can be creative. Among the must-have skills, I include public speaking.

The means needs to satisfy the why.

In a moment of frustration, after poor presentations by persons unable to explain a topic they know very well, I decided to put in place public speaking training for all staff members in the business unit.

"There is no budget," HR stated.

"There is no time," the director said.

Based on the constraints, I devised a plan for which no excuses could be made. That was a strong advantage of working in a holacracy: as I was able to prove that my project was good for the company, I could go for it. To facilitate the delivery of courses, I created an online platform using existing content material that was available, to which I added some more. I developed a methodology for the modules so they would be divided into several categories. As exercise is the most important element in learning, I used my knowledge experience sharing and organised groups of four to eight participants. I convinced some talented people in public speaking to coach those sessions, while paying attention to finding a balance between men and women, native speakers in Dutch, French, other languages, from different departments.... I provided them with basic training on how to animate groups and shared the methodology. Over a few months, participants were meeting every month for two hours to experience their presentation skills and exchange. Then, they tested it in "real life", and came back a month later to improve it. In one year, more than 150 employees were trained. The training was even rated as superior to a two-day course by some participants. Experiencing this in a "safe space" on a regular basis was helping to improve the practice. There was no mobilisation for a few days: two hours can always be found in a month. No cash was spent, everything was done internally. Additionally, since the groups were structured so that they were not composed of people who worked daily together, a sense of cohesion was created amongst the teams. This was an unintended indirect consequence. This kind of formula can be applied to any skills if you want to ensure a sustainable impact. With classic training, people forget 60% after a few days, and the rate decreases with time[44]. On top of feeling the learning, information should be repeated to be retained.

To learn, you must listen. Really listen. The value of a conversation will be lost if you are just passively acknowledging and thinking about your to do list or dinner. Research shows astonishing numbers: we keep only 20 to 50% of what we hear[45]. Don't be angry if your partner does not remember everything you said; you would probably do the same. One can expect that the low percentage kept consists of the most important elements. Well, no. If I must think about a very nice conference I attended, a big part is about the clothes of the lady presenting (which were really nice), the too warm room, the food. Therefore, we all need to improve our active listening skills: to get information, to understand, to learn. Active listening consists in making a conscious effort to hear the complete message being transmitted, not just the words (or the clothes). It requires a lot of focus and energy. That is why psychologists don't interrupt, except for repeating the words expressed, which, by the way, helps them to maintain their concentration. When the person has finished, then you can comment, ask questions, summarise, agree, or disagree. Our productivity and human interactions will only be enriched. Isabel Verstraete has evaluated the collaboration on companies, the poor result is due to a lack of listening.

"Companies only scored 46% on collaboration because people don't listen[46]. Collaboration can only happen when there is psychological safety. A lot of CEOs like to listen, but they're not very good at hearing."
Isabel Verstraete

Ilham Kadri built her Diversity, Equity and Inclusion roadmap, "Solvay One Dignity", on listening, which enabled her to hear the real issues to address. Employees were asked about their opinions and ideas through a hackathon. They found, for instance, that LGBTQ+ employees don't feel at ease being their true selves at work; that female employees, non-European employees, and employees with fewer educational degrees struggle to access career opportunities.

Like any development, self-awareness is essential. The first step of an improvement journey is to understand your own personal style of communication. My most successful training is "inter-personal communication", where participants understand themselves. Only then can you start understanding others and up-grade your skills. Francis Blake also believes that self-awareness is a necessary quality of a business leader, which derives from active listening.

"As a leader, you need first to know yourself very well: where do you come from, what are your biases, what is your background, what is your education, what are you good and not good at? The more you know yourself, the more you will be without fear when someone else comes with another idea. This will help you find in your organisation the people thinking differently. Then give them the freedom to express their opinion."
Francis Blake

Unconsciously biased

Have you ever wondered what your biases are? We all have biases. Denying them is counterproductive. Ask yourself: on the road, do you tend to be harder if an older woman is in the driver's seat? When you are renting your house, do you say "no" more easily to people with a foreign accent? Do you have more crushes on people resembling you? When hiring, do you provide more negative feedback to people who are overweight?

We are biased, depending on our education, our country/region/city/neighbour-hood culture, our professional culture, our experiences. As an example, when I was sixteen years old, a neighbour, Gérald, came to my door yelling at me, and since I did not react, he asked with specific signs if I spoke French. Actually, I was very sick, and my parents were at work. I did not understand what he wanted; my fever was occupying me completely. When I realised that it was an aggression, I demanded that he leave our doorstep, and if he did not, I would contact the police. At that moment, he understood that I spoke French. Later my father explained to me that the guy was the hysterical person who had made a scene a year earlier, when my parents visited the land for the first time. My grandmother, God grant her eternal rest, was sick in the car and had to sit on the grass while my parents were visiting the property. Upon seeing them, he called the police, ran out of his house, rang all the nearby houses, and screamed: "The Arabs are coming here to steal everything from us! Look, she is establishing a camp here!" The police officers were nice; they told them, "Welcome to our neighbourhood. Don't pay attention to this guy." My parents worked all their life to construct their dream house; they spent years looking for a suitable piece of land, and they found it in Waterloo, a rich suburb in the Brussels area. There was no way they would allow anyone to interfere with their dream, so they went on with the purchase of the plot. To compound matters, my cat chased the birds he fed every day. "Look, even their cat is a savage; it is eating my birds!" Gérald shouted to the entire district. It took my parents several months to set the record straight, so that he began to become less aggressive. He was sometimes pleasant, but his old demons would suddenly take possession of him once again. During a construction problem, he provided us with water and electricity, and then got angry when the wind brought a tree branch to his side. At some point, he shared his story with my father. (Remember what I said at the beginning: my father is an excellent listener.)

He owned several apartments in the centre of Brussels, a neighbourhood that has fallen into disrepair over the years. Some renters were not paying him. Once, he went to them to request his due. They tied him to a chair and beat him mercilessly. It was the first time that he had been in contact with a person of colour.

My father's empathy made Gérald feel sufficiently at ease to disclose painful parts of his life. When we heard about his sad story, we were shocked. Although this could not justify his actions, we could understand his almost natural aggression towards any foreigners as a survival instinct. The problem does not only stem from the violent people who assaulted him, but also from the fact that at the age of 60, he had never lived with diversity of appearance. So, he assimilated one bad action with a skin colour. Basic racism. When we moved to go back to Brussels, he was sad. We were "very nice neighbours, good Arabs". I just hoped he would meet more people of colour before the end of his life, so that he would not see us as "the exceptions". I do not know if you have already expressed this type of comment, but please understand my profound unease when someone tells me, "Yes, but that is you. You are an exception. You are not the same." The same as who? An exception to what, a pattern of evilness? Of course, I am not the same. Nobody is the same. We are all different. That is our richness. And the difference is not always apparent.

"We live in times where some people tend to push for a vision about one's own identity understood so differently than the identity of other groups that actually, they come to think that the survival or the flourishing of their own identity becomes dependent on their ability to impede others from developing their own identity. This should alarm us."
Isabelle Ferreras

Vulnerability is strong

Knowing oneself is also about accepting your vulnerability. Some years ago, I joined the board of an organisation. In the first meeting, I mainly listened. I spent many days reading and analysing the documents. When asked for my advice, I replied, "I don't know. I need to think more about it. For now, I rely on my colleagues' judgements." I felt overwhelmed by the amount of information and unable to decide. I was not sure about anything, certainly not about my answer. "Maybe I should not have said that, but simply that I agree and that's it." Later on, a colleague told me, "I thought your answer was very brave. I have been here for many years, and I often found myself lost, but I never dared to say it. To avoid feeling ashamed, I appeared to understand everything. I felt stupid instead. When I heard you give this answer, I was impressed, I thought: Wow, she is so honest and reliable." Another team member told me, "You are so self-confident. I envy that."

My doubts did not make me weak, on the contrary, they made me strong.

My doubts did not make me weak, on the contrary, they made me strong. After a few board meetings, I felt that I had enough knowledge to actively participate. My husband challenged me. He said that I had had enough knowledge since the beginning:

to get to that board, I had passed exams with the highest score. If I was not skilled enough, I wouldn't have. Was it my imposter syndrome that made me hesitant? Well, maybe. But being humble is not something to regret, rather to uphold.

A leader has a responsibility towards others. He or she must strive for impact. Pierre Gurdjian has developed a leadership model based on impact, legacy, and brilliance.

"I like to look at Leadership as an invitation rather than as a defined set of attributes. An invitation to discover, experience and grow. A never-ending process of psychodynamic development. A journey to impact and wisdom.

I also like to distinguish three complementary themes for such a journey: Brilliance, Impact and Legacy:
- *Brilliance: discovering what our own individual "sweet spot" of unique strengths is*
- *Impact: acting with courage to change reality with lucidity for the unavoidable counter-reaction triggered by any action*
- *Legacy: realising that what ultimately matters is what we leave behind..."*

Pierre Gurdjian

What strikes me about his principle is the legacy part. Do you think about what will be said about you when you die? What actions will endure when you are gone? Well, I think about it a lot; that's certainly why I am so invested in societal initiatives. When I was promoted to head of a department, my n+1 asked me about my next step. Being a director, developing greater scope, having more people in the team? The truth is, I did not care about that. Working toward a meaningful cause while having fun was a priority for me. Besides flattering my ego, what is the benefit of this kind of job? I considered my legacy: "Ihsane Haouach, a beloved director." That's not very exciting, is it? Explaining that this type of progression was not relevant to me was difficult. On the contrary, working with diverse people and building together something innovative and impactful provides positive energy. You can be a worker, an employee, a manager, a director, a CEO: what good have you done at your position that will last?

There is a temptation to take only short-term actions: we may still collect compliments. They can, however, disappear as soon as we leave. To invest in long-term impact, we must have a profound desire to make the company better and learn from our past failures. In assessing her previous accomplishments, Ilham Kadri evaluates them with humility and is committed to enhancing the sustainability of her actions by doing things differently.

—

"In all the companies I led in my career, Diversity, Equity and Inclusion was part of the sustainability roadmap, but the reality is, I always failed in building a DEI environment. When I look back, DEI was not sticky. With Solvay, I'm trying to do it differently. I focus on building equity first and creating the right inclusive environment to attract and retain diverse talents. People need to feel respected, welcomed, heard, valued, and therefore they will be more engaged, more innovative, perform at their best and stay with you. If you don't listen to diversity, diversity leaves you, and the best leave you first."

Ilham Kadri

—

After I had only been head of a department for a few months, one of the team members, Samuel, approached me with the idea of resigning. He had an offer from a competitor, to which he had applied before I took the role. At that time, he was unhappy because of a promotion promised and not given. One of the first fights I had with my n+1 and n+2 was for him: I wanted to correct the last year's mistake. Now that he had his promotion, he was talking of leaving. I was embarrassed because of my efforts. It is true that my credibility would take a hit. I asked him more about the proposal. It was interesting, not only for the money. He said that if I asked him to refuse it, he would. Obviously, I wanted to convince him to stay, and I tried until I realised how selfish it was. I asked: "Do you want it?" "Yes," he answered. "Then take it. I am not your mother; I am your manager. You are allowed to leave me if you find a better offer. My role is first to support the development of the team members. Of course, your departure will be tricky, of course you will be missed, of course it will be hard to hire someone else. But that is professional life. Maybe one day we will work together again. Just follow your own path."

Then he promised to help me find a replacement. I told him I would not replace him; each person brings something else, even to the same role. I have seen many managers considering a departure as a treason. I once said to a director: "Even in marriage, there is divorce. If not done with maturity, it can become very ugly." He was complaining about an employee leaving him, "with everything" he had "done for her". Please, stop this. First, he had not done it only for her but also for him, for the company, for the other teammates... Secondly, even so, so what? You help others, they help you, does this mean you are linked until death do you part? Accepting that people fly with their own wings is part of being a good leader. Accepting that people do not make the same choices as you is part of being an inclusive leader.

Intuitively inclusive

I have met many leaders; each have their own style, then they complete it with learning experiences. Inclusion is a natural part of leadership for some individuals, such as Thibaut Georgin. Working with him, I have seen how inclusiveness comes naturally to him. That is why he considers himself a novice rather than an expert. Because he is intuitively open, he does not need to work on it or pay attention every time.

"For the moment, I'm working in some public companies, and there, the political dimension is present. I try not to be obsessed and blinded by those differences. I take the time to talk to others, even if they are not from the same political sensitivity, or French-speakers or Flemish. I don't have really the feeling to force myself."
Thibaut Georgin

Whether they are apparent or not, there are many barriers that cause us to feel different. Curiosity is a powerful enabler of diversity, except when it triggers questions of justification, which inhibit it. A nuance exists between getting close to someone and then asking questions to gain a better understanding of them, rather than directly questioning them, sometimes before even saying "hi".

—

Whether they are apparent or not, there are many barriers that cause us to feel different.

—

At a professional networking event, a woman approached me and bombarded me with numerous questions. First, I attempted to answer, then I viewed the scene as an external observer (disassociation can be helpful in some situations), and I ceased. My response was, "I am sorry, but who are you, and who do you think you are to demand personal and political opinions? In fact, you did not even ask for my name or introduce yourself to me." To which she replied, "Well, if I need to hire you, I need to know your opinions on these matters." "First, no, you do not need to know the views of all your employees regarding protests in Iran and working conditions in Qatar. Are you even operating a business there? Second, did I ask you anything? Do you think I would ever apply for a job where the boss is so judgmental and aggressive?" She looked disconcerted. Two other women smiled at me. I chose to leave her before the situation degenerated. On my way out, a person of foreign origin told me, "There was a strange woman at the event. I do not understand what she wanted from me. She asked me about political matters, but I have no expertise in international politics. I kept telling her what my competencies were, and she did not stop."

One could say that I should always engage, and effect change through dialogue. That may be true in most cases, but with time, I have come to sense when a person has an open attitude, and when she does not. Investing time and energy in individuals who will only hear what they want to hear is not necessary. This can result in more harm than good, as they will take all your enthusiasm. This faulty example was the result of misplaced curiosity. Nevertheless, well-intended curiosity is a way to be open, and it is even at the heart of diversity.

Inclusion is not natural for everyone. Regardless of who you are, your actions have an impact on others. In some cases, you may not be aware of how you affect others. I had to demonstrate to a team member the effect of his bad mood on the team. That guy was nice, friendly. But when something did not go his way, professionally or privately, he would blow up and get anxious about stupid things. All the team would be impacted: there would be no discussions or laughter in the open space; the atmosphere would become heavy. Once he became aware of his impact, he immediately adapted his behaviour. A leader observes and then helps people improve. Hence, constructive feedback is key. Don't be too hard on yourself: we all make mistakes. Embrace your vulnerability.

"How I feel invariably translates to how I treat other people. Making sure that I'm in a place of gratitude, acceptance, contentment, and fulfilment makes me a better leader. If I'm empathic towards myself, I can be a lot more empathetic towards others. I was harsh on myself up until recently. If you are not in a good place yourself, it's hard to be a good colleague, a good manager, a good coach."
Mikaël Wornoo

Admitting one's faults and acting on them requires courage. As opposed to what might be intuitively believed, knowing one's weaknesses can build self-confidence. Accepting oneself is the first step towards accepting others. Only then, one will be able to empathise with colleagues, which is a prerequisite to helping them grow.

> **"** *To be courageous ... requires no exceptional qualifications, no magic formula, no special combination of time, place, and circumstance. It is an opportunity that sooner or later is presented to us all.* **"**
> **John F. Kennedy**

Role modelling

A non-inclusive board of directors will set the frame for the whole organisation: once the norms are defined, it is hard to dismantle. This is where role models are useful. I have often found myself called a role model; maybe you have too. In the beginning, I felt uncomfortable: high pressure is placed on your shoulders, you cannot fail, you must deserve a title you never sought. With time, I have come to accept it, since I believe that everyone can serve as a role model in some manner. Ilham Kadri is clearly considered as a role model. Nevertheless, the fact that she is systematically described on the basis of her origins and gender is not always easy to accept. It is limiting to identify someone as only being a "woman of colour". Her difference lies more in her leadership style than in her appearance.

"The headlines were: 'First woman CEO at Solvay. Triple glass ceiling break.' It was so funny. They forgot that I had already been a CEO in the USA. The biggest difference was my professional background compared to the previous Solvay leaders. But women are still an anecdote – hopefully a good one – but we're still an anecdote. The statistics are so sobering, that the first thing you see is the woman, the woman of colour, with African origin, not coming from this type of school, basically a non-white male with white hair. It is just a symptom of the problem. The good news is that if they talk about us, and if I can give that dream to a little girl in Casablanca, or Mumbai, or Molenbeek, or Atlanta, Georgia, that's great. If this can help the switch from 'This is not for me' to 'If she can do it, I can do it too', you made my day!"
Ilham Kadri

Depending on your area of expertise, your exposure, your influence, your actions, you can have an impact on others, and leave that legacy Pierre Gurdjian was referring to. We do not need to be superheroes, but just do the right things at the right moments in the right ways. Ibrahim Ouassari knows his role-model potential and uses it to deconstruct stereotypes against... experienced white men. He deplores that people from minorities have many diplomas but not yet enough experience to get better jobs.

"Sometimes I take youngsters with me to meetings with big companies. They see guys above 50 years old in suits talking to me in a very nice way. They would see the same man in a recruitment interview, they would be impressed, and now they see the human being beyond the role.

Diversity is not just to have people on some functions, it needs to be in higher functions with decision power. We have Ilham Kadri, but we need more."
Ibrahim Ouassari

In contrast, Ilham begs minorities to get out of a defeatist condition and take a seat at the table, following her grandmother's advice. However, not everyone has the natural strength to break ice ceilings. Personally, I feel like a minority in appearance, but not necessarily in mind when contributing to a decision for instance.

"I hope women and minorities are going to stop feeling sorry for themselves. I've never felt like I'm a victim. When I enter a room, trust me, I don't feel like I'm a minority. I'm a leader full stop. The woman part doesn't come through. I am here and I have my seat at the table. That's what my grandmother told me: have a seat at the table and speak up."
Ilham Kadri

I've always tried to have a seat at the table. Sometimes, however, it is necessary to envision leaving the table to bring about a fundamental change.

Have a seat to leave the table

When there is a reorganisation, top management often organises workshops in order to involve operational personnel in the process. The thing is... they are not always listened to. In the event that a large consulting firm is involved and has a thorough understanding of the target organisation, you may wish to focus only on those ideas that are similar to that of the consulting firm. That is something I have seen too many times in my years in change management. I once felt so unheard that I went for a walk to see the ducks instead. At least, it was clear I was talking to myself. It was during a seminar, in a beautiful place surrounded by trees and water. I was tired of expressing my concerns, repeatedly. I joined the workshop believing that our branch unit could be transformed based on societal challenges: energy transition, diversity, equity, inclusion. Those principles were present on paper but absent in the discussions. Desperate, I left for a walk. A colleague based in Italy joined me. He said, "They have no idea what they are talking about. They have no idea what it is to work outside their ivory tower in Paris." I was surprised: my thoughts were so obvious? I smiled and continued to look at the ducks. A swan arrived. Then two others. We were observing their dynamics, the behavioural change with the arrival of a new being. Another colleague, based in Latin America, joined us. He complained, "I knew my trip would be useless." I looked at them and realised: I am not alone. Those guys were not speaking. They were watching the discussions unfolding. I began to wonder: is there a silenced majority? Or even a significant silenced minority disagreeing with the direction taken?

Lunch time arrived. As we left, swans and ducks were silently sharing the place. The human resources director came to me. "I understand your concern, but you cannot change it all. Step by step." I answered that I did not know if I could be more patient, because I did not see any significant advancement taken. Agreed actions did not match the presented goal at all. This was complete and utter nonsense. She tried to convince me. I listened to her but cordially disagreed. Back in the room, I stepped up, expecting to be supported. "I fully disagree with the current orientation. Some key elements are missing. If those cannot be addressed, it is okay, but then it will be better if I leave. I cannot co-sign this output that is so far away from the ambitions announced." I explained point by point, with some non-prepared arguments. With my deep values, a lot of emotion was being exposed to a large audience. My voice trembled, and my cheeks turned red. I did my best to control them, as emotions would have discredited me – as a young woman, you easily can be seen as "a naïve idealist, too sensitive". The two accomplices jumped in and expressed their agreement with me. Then others spoke as well. The silenced participants started to speak up. We were still a minority. But somehow, our assertive demonstration showed how serious the topic was to us. It was not a "nice to have", but a "must have", we insisted.

The room was quiet for a few minutes. Then a member of the board took the point: "They are right. We are really missing this." Suddenly, all agreed. I think that if he had not been there and if he had not supported our ideas, we would have left, frustrated but coherent. Whatever a board member does, says, or does not say has an impact on the full organisation. It means that as a director, people in the company take you more seriously. So, use it for good. Ask your people about their opinions and actively listen to them. Francis Blake explained how it has helped them overreach their performance objectives. Hanan Challouki and Mikaël Wornoo also insist on the power of a conversation and advise listening carefully, to be able to evaluate yourself and detect areas for improvement.

"Most human interactions go wrong because of a lack of empathy. Initiate conversations with people on different levels. The top too often stays at the top. Don't act based what you believe is inclusive, but on the correct insights."
Hanan Challouki

"If you want your organisation to be to noted for inclusiveness, ask your people how they would rate it. Have a one-to-one conversation with the people that you expect feel excluded. The best way to empathise is to hear their stories. Try to discover if that is the same way that you are experiencing – probably not. Things will come up that you can implement right away."
Mikaël Wornoo

Storytelling helps to change things, because it appeals to empathy: you listen, imagine, feel, live what the other has experienced. Our human brain is more activated by stories than by facts[47]. The tool is powerful, whether it is for conflict resolution, marketing, influencing, making complex decisions in meetings. I cannot stand inefficient meetings. In my previous role as a change agent, I led a workshop on meeting efficiency. I realised it was about more than just efficiency; it was also about inclusion. The preparation of a meeting is evidently beneficial for everyone involved, as it provides ample opportunities for everyone to consider and prepare their ideas, suggestions, and actions, or simply who should and should not attend. Nevertheless, it is especially helpful for introverted or socially anxious employees since preparation time enhances their confidence. This makes it easier for them to express their opinions to others. Additionally, if some team members are not native speakers of the language used in the meeting, preparation will help ensure that they are able to understand what is being said.

" To know that we know what we know, and to know that we do not know, that is true knowledge. "
Nicolaus Copernicus

Evaluation

Once you have implemented some initiatives, then comes the hard exercise of evaluation. In order to manage, you need to know the facts. It is however complicated to establish KPIs and measure them. Kay Formanek[48], an author and expert in diversity and inclusion, listed what she considered as "the vital signs of diversity and how they manifest:

- A negative trend in employee engagement pulse surveys
- Unstable rates of retention for minorities relative to the overall population
- Job offer declines, particularly by minorities
- Benefit gaps for minorities versus the rest of the population

- Grievances on unconscious or systemic bias
- Inclusive leadership rating decline
- Shrinking minority representation per level, location, business units
- Negative feedback on diversity from customers and suppliers
- Promotion gaps for minorities versus the rest of the population
- Distribution of line, imbalance in minority representation in positions holding more responsibility, authority, and higher compensation.[49]"

Those past few years, more and more indexes appear to measure DEI in an organisation. Some have gathered into a community committed to sharing strategies for measuring representation and fair pay, Catalyst[50], stating that "What Gets Measured Gets Managed". They assess three values:
- Percentage of representation on an organisation's board
- Percentage of representation by employment category
- The ratio of compensation by employee category (e.g., equal pay for equal work)

Although the focus is on women equality, the indicator can be applied for broader objectives. Ilham Kadri investigated the pay gap in her company, published the results and committed to resolve it.

"We needed to measure the undesired pay gap between men and women and different categories of our employees. I didn't know if there were any! When we announced our plan and shared that we have a pay gap, I said "It's wrong, but this is not the end of the story. There is a gap and I'm going to work on it."
Ilham Kadri

Isabel Verstraete has developed a tool to evaluate the implementation of the CARE principles[51] with a market research agency, consisting of an inquiry of 40 questions about how employees perceive their organisation. The tested companies score poorly at 51% for diversity. If you want to develop a new way, an internal audit is a good step: know your organisation and detect the elements to keep and the elements to improve.

> **❝** *I'm optimistic about technology. Not because I believe in technology, but because I believe in people and humanity.* **❞** **Sundar Pichai**

Thierry Geerts is aligned with the mindset of Sundar Pichai, his CEO, and sees digitalisation as a very strong tool for inclusion. However, data privacy for one will not allow you to monitor everything you want.

"Imagine only twenty years ago, an encyclopaedia was something quite expensive, only rich people would have it at home. Today, 95% of the Belgians have access to it! Being connected create inclusive possibilities. It is for learning, for knowledge, for getting in touch with your loved ones and feeling included, without getting disconnected with your roots. Digitalisation is helping inclusion, but it is just a tool, it will not solve the problem like a magical stick. Fifty years ago, if you would have loved to be included, we could have said, 'Well, it's complicated.' Today we have everything on the table; it is just the place of everyone and our leaders to make sure that it is happening. It is possible and it is needed."
Thierry Geerts

Diversity is a reality in society. The question is: how do you ensure that inclusiveness is part of the DNA of your organisation? You probably won't do it alone or all at once. Any change requires time, but keep in mind that some of your people are suffering as a result of the current situation. Indulge yourself, but don't forget to indulge your colleagues who are in need as well. It is necessary to combine short-term measures to relieve part of the burden on these individuals with long-term systemic transformation.

——

"There is no silver bullet: lots of actions need to be done in sync. As defined in your model, you need patience and empathy. Patience because it's a long-term engagement, not only for me but also for my successor. It takes a generation to change things. I need the pipeline to build all of this to enable that inclusive culture. I'm impatient by nature, but I need to have empathy for myself because it's going to take longer than one mandate and one CEO. I also need to have empathy for others: some people may be suffering inside the organisation, while others are victims of unconscious bias. It takes more than one training session because it's part of our education."

Ilham Kadri

——

In the end, it all boils down to being open, patient, empathic and natural…

Natural

Find the space in which you are both yourself.

Natural

is the inherent sense of one's personality, expressed through effortless endeavour.

There is an issue that I am working on, but that keeps coming up: I speak too quickly. This is the natural way in which I express myself. I am a fast thinker, easily bored. This is not practical when I have to speak in public. If I do not control my speed, people lose track of what I am saying. Additionally, it poses a challenge to leadership: one of my best managers, Jeroen, told me, "Ihsane, stop." You take a high-speed train when people are on a regular train. Stop and check regularly that everyone is with you, so that you don't wait in the dock when you arrive at your destination." When presenting to management committees (with, as usual, mainly white men around fifty years old), rapid responses were unconsciously perceived as not being "well-considered enough", and thus not credible. A piece of valuable advice he gave me was to "count until three before answering". Of course, I had to count slowly.

In the early stages of my career, I was not taken seriously by a manager. I was preparing risk reporting, but apparently too quickly. My papers were not even examined by him, yet he demanded, "You should check it again". Having already verified them, I did not understand what he expected me to do. I asked a senior team member for her opinion. She reviewed my analysis and confirmed its accuracy. She advised: "Well, don't send it too quickly." Following that, I began to deliver my reports one or two days after finishing them, and to assist her without alerting the manager. It was a win-win situation: I learned so much from her and she got free help. The manager was so disconnected from his team that he never knew it.

The fact that I made efforts to speak more slowly and deliver reports later didn't change me, however, it adapted my natural working style.

The natural relief

Mikaël Wornoo felt only at 23 years old what it was to be himself outside family environment.

"I grew up in a very white neighbourhood. There are many subtle cultural differences that I associated more with family than the African culture. The first time I was surrounded by a bunch of black people, we were laughing at the same things, we had the same mannerisms, the same way of carrying ourselves. I felt seen, that they really understood me. It was such a relief. I did not have to hide certain parts of my personality. I realise what it could do in terms of wellbeing. That's when I started caring about DEI."
Mikaël Wornoo

Personally, I had a similar track to Mikaël. I discovered diversity at university. I was in an elite school with kids who did not look like me, so I felt that I could not belong. The socio-economic difference helped dig the gap. I was raised in a family with an average income, while many students in my class came from well-off families. When the teacher said, "You need to ask your parents to give 250 euros for our next trip, by the end of the week," it was a lot for me. I did not even want to say it to my parents, as I knew they would have to sacrifice other expenses for them, for me. The other kids did not seem to be concerned. There is a similar effect when it comes to clothing: when you are not able to use the same baskets and bags, you feel different. What I did then is to assert my difference: instead of denying it, it became a statement. My pride felt it was in control, while it was only a reaction. Of course, in those situations, everyone is losing.

"You can have a beautiful outfit, you can have a scarf, you can have great makeup and still wear another costume and hide behind your true self. The belief is that when there is dignity and inclusiveness, when you have that open organisation, when you feel free and safe, then you can bring your whole self to work and thrive."
Ilham Kadri

Open to be natural, natural to be open

The challenge is to be open while staying natural, to find a common safe space.

There is a clear tension between Openness and Natural, which enables the model to be complete. The challenge is to be open while staying natural, to find a common safe space.

"If you are two very different people from different backgrounds, how do you get to engage with each other? I remember a guy who didn't want to shake hands with women. I felt like it was a way to treat me differently from men.

There can be an intrinsic paradox: trying to be patient, open, empathetic, which is maybe not your natural self? What are the limits, what are your core values? In your framework, Openness for me is more about the fact that as a society we need to agree on the basis for discussion, Natural is more for me individually."

Audrey Hanard

"I think you must correct yourself. If you say to a 60-year-old white man who has managed a company for decades with 100% of the shares: 'Be natural, be yourself,' then you will not change anything. We can blame the guy, but we can also be empathic: that is his world view. The point is, maybe you have been misled because it is something else that is successful for your company."

Thierry Geerts

Be natural, be yourself: from where to where? I have struggled with this question all my life. Being in different environments, I feel that I always need to make an effort to cope with people. It is tiring to feel like you are different and need to pay attention to cultural codes linked to various professional environments (still, I love having a foot in different worlds).

Sometimes it is not even conscious. For instance, a friend transforms his voice when talking to his colleagues: he uses a high-pitched voice, while a deeper one with his friends. He did not realise it, neither did he recognise it when mentioned...

When I was living in Hungary, I wanted to be with the local people. I did not want to be like those expatriates, thinking that their way of life is better and therefore not mixing with a "race" that is "beneath" them. Only, alcohol was a common part of their life. They could for instance share a palinka, a traditional fruit spirit, on Monday at 8 o'clock, as a "How did your weekend go?" "I went to my grand-mother, and she gave me this palinka she distilled, reaching an alcohol content of 70%!". They will drink it in a nanosecond and go on with their work, as if they had drunk a glass of juice. As part of my values, I choose not to drink alcohol. How-ever, I still wanted to share nice informal moments with them. Notwithstanding the mass of personal and professional information exchanged, this is also part of my values: being human, caring for the people I collaborate with. On the one side, my value of not consuming alcohol; on the other side, my value of befriending my colleagues, topped off by my professional need to fit in. So, what could I do? Something Belgian citizens are good at: the art of compromise. I accepted going to places I did not feel comfortable in, while never holding a glass of alcohol in my hand. I agreed to cheer with my orange juice. I agreed to not eat at some evenings, because the only dish served was not halal, yet explaining my reasons. I knew it was hard for them to understand all the differences: I was the only Muslim and Arab person they had ever met, and one of the rare expatriates they let in. They started to find places where vegetarian dishes were served and warned me if any alcohol was put in a meal (it is amazing how it was present, even in candies and chocolates...). I opened myself to their ways while remaining myself.

If I was completely natural, it would not have worked.
If I had conceded my core values, it would not have worked.

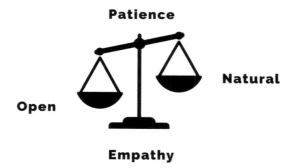

A constant balance between being open and being natural must be found. It is where inclusivity comes (and not integration, and certainly not assimilation. It is about both you and the others adjusting one another). I am not the only one who has gone through these challenges. Satish Kumar and his friend Menon travelled around the world while staying vegetarian and not touching money. One evening, they were invited to a party thrown in their honour, where their host had slaughtered two goats. They were embarrassed, *"My goodness! Two goats have been slaughtered for two vegetarian pacifists."* They hesitated between politeness and adherence to their principles. They did not wish to hurt their hosts' feelings, yet they remembered their promises and explained gently that they were flattered but could not eat it. *"We do not wish to offend you or reject your generosity, but please understand that according to our commitment to non-violence, we cannot eat meat. We see that you have plenty of fried rice, vegetables, yogurt, and cheese – this is more than enough. But please enjoy this delicacy of tender meat yourselves".* With such delicacy, their host could only understand.[52]

Of course, we all have limits. Those limits are set by the individuals themselves and not subject to a decision on their behalf. There is a risk when assuming a limit for somebody: you can be completely wrong. Ilham Kadri had the experience with women site leaders. Management often supposes that "it is not a job for them", hence discriminated against them with a good (paternalistic) intention.

"You need to ask the question before a woman with children refuses a position with more responsibilities. If they have the competency and the desire to do it, those women will say, 'Don't worry about my life, I'm going to manage my kids and my personal life. Ask me the question and then it's up to me to pick up the job or not.'"
Ilham Kadri

" *I often had the impression of being an alibi for women. Everywhere I went, I heard: 'But yes, we have given women a voice since there is Simone Veil.'* **"** **Simone Veil**

To be in, or not to be

Change agents are often faced with the dilemma of whether they should participate in an assembly whose values do not align with their own: accept with hope or
decline participation with protest. The choice is not easy. The first strategy relies
on positive thinking. You believe that those people are capable of changing. Take a
case of a person of colour nominated to an exposed and strategic position in an organisation willing to show their inclusiveness as a facade. You know it and accept
the job. Your willingness to serve as their moral caution is not merely motivated
by the advantages offered on a social and economic level, but you believe that
your natural presence can induce them to be more open, patient, and empathic.

The second strategy is more radical. Because the basis for the nomination is not
there for you, you decline the nomination. The situation appears hypocritical to
you, and you do not wish to be a part of it. There are three options available to you
at this point: to make a public statement, to make demands that may be accepted,
or to remain silent and move on. Depending on the organisation and the context,
one strategy is more suitable than the others. I used both, mainly the first one.
This did not exempt me from reminding them that if I was there only because of
my photogenic face and all my proposed changes were blocked, I would leave (and
not necessarily quietly). Audrey Hanard shares a dilemma she encountered.

"I had a request to speak at a business club open only to male members.
Accepting the offer, or not, made me question my values about inclu-
siveness. When reflecting, though, I realised that there are clubs open
only to women too, and somehow that 'feels' different because that's
a minority trying to regroup to build power. Then, I wondered: who is
'allowed' to meet separately and who is not? It becomes quite complex."
Audrey Hanard

Ibrahim Ouassari also found himself in a similar situation. Except that he answered positively to the invitation for an event but refused to be a member if no woman was allowed, even though he would be the first of foreign origin. He applied both strategies.

> *"I was invited to a men's business club, and they asked: 'Do you think there is still discrimination in Belgium?' I answered that they should look around. They said that everyone is welcome in their club. That is not enough. People have to want to come. If it was more inclusive, they would be interested in being here. I try to make them aware that in today's Belgium, it's strange to find ourselves in a single community. They accepted the criticism."*
> **Ibrahim Ouassari**

I wonder if they accept criticism generally, or only from "an exception": a man with a worldwide positive reputation who speaks their language.

Productive discrimination

Positive discrimination (also called affirmative action) and quotas are sometimes counterproductive. A friend shared his despair with me: he needed to recruit a new marketing director, he looked for a suitable candidate, and one was great. In light of his previous director's outstanding performance, the bar was set very high. The headquarters did not even want to interview the candidate: "No, we need a woman." He reacted as if it was my doing and said very angrily, "This is discrimination against men. Is this what you want?" I quietly answered "No". He did not expect this answer, so his silence gave me the opportunity to elaborate. "I do not think demanding a woman and ignoring men is the right way. But (yes, there is always a "but") asking to try to have a woman to join a mainly male board is the right way. How was the job communicated? Did it circulate widely? Did you also interview female candidates or did only men apply?". His response surprised me, although it should not have, as it happens frequently: "No, we did not publish the job opening, we just looked at our network and this guy matches fully, so we did not even need to spend money and time on this." Well... do you see the problem? Just as the headquarters was wrong to blindly impose the nomination of a woman, this director was wrong in his attempt to recruit. Without proper broad communication, how can you go beyond your environment with persons similar to you, to find diversity both in appearance and in profile?

The good news is that by setting this criterion, the CEO and HR are forced to expand the field of possibilities and to look outside their current environment. The bad news is that, thanks to this affirmative action, the person nominated can be seen, or see herself, as illegitimate. This can discredit any wonderful work the person may do. Then, she will need to work more for less recognition, but she is probably used to the effects of the imposter syndrome.

The criteria themselves may sometimes be problematic. If you create a job description based on existing functioning, you will be looking for candidates with similar profiles to the current director. Different candidates will not even apply, and if they do, recruiters will probably exclude them on the basis that their profile does not match. Be aware of bias in a job description. A more open recruitment process is necessary if you wish to recruit diverse candidates.

Even a leader as brilliant as Audrey Hanard needed positive discrimination.

"In some cases, I was supported because of these inclusion criteria. I brought the right skills, experience, and I also happened to be a woman. For example, my appointment as chair of the Friday group[53]: the former chair saw that I was actively engaged and thought having me as his successor would be a great signal to women, who were fewer in number at the time. It was not just because I was a woman – which would have been an issue – but it contributed. I do believe that this proactive process in favour of diversity does counterbalance other missed opportunities, where people might not have thought of you, not deliberately, but because you were less close to them than male peers."

Audrey Hanard

Indeed, it tempers the effects of negative experiences.

A colleague once came to me with the same dilemma:

- "Should I accept the promotion? I know that it is because I am a woman," she said.
- "No Marie, it is not because you are a woman; it is because you are the best person for the job. Being a woman is only part of the argument. Would they have proposed it if you had not been working in the team for ten years and performed very well? And even so... please! How many times did you not get that promotion because you are a woman...? Do not refuse an opportunity, because when it is not presented, you have no choice," I replied.

We should not turn away an open hand, because we cannot afford to refuse opportunities when some are not even presented. Positive discrimination triggers a shift from the unconscious bias of systematically recruiting a man to a conscious one: recruiting a woman. This change of paradigm could be applied to all diversity aspects: background, religion, handicap, nationality, sexual orientation... and profiles. If Ibrahim Ouassari strongly pushes for quotas, he insists on the time limit.

"There are some quotas for women. I would like the same for other minorities. When I look at my daughter, she is ambitious but that's not the case for other youngsters from African origins or with a disability. But quotas need to be provisory. When we reach equality, we remove them."
Ibrahim Ouassari

Equity is like perfection: we must strive for it and accept its unattainability.

Unfortunately, equity will never be reached. It is like perfection: we must strive for it and accept its unattainability. You can work in phases: for two years, we fix quotas for gender equality, then foreign background, then religious culture, then introverted people... Of course, you will not force your people to pass a personality test, but generally, people love them. Data can be anonymised to build statistics. With a bit of training, you can easily detect a profile type (be careful, however, not to put people in a box too quickly; we are so much more than what we show). From those analyses, you can decide to put an emphasis on profile in recruitments, on top of appearances, and obviously... experience and skills.

"We don't have quotas at the end of the recruitment process, but we do at the beginning. Interviews cannot start if we don't have a diverse slate of candidates according to several KPIs. It does not always lead to the results hoped for but at least we actively push ourselves. I don't believe in blind CV approaches, where the idea is that if you just remove all unconscious biases, it will work out. It's not true because some people will self-select out from the start of the process. I do also believe in meritocracy. You don't want to end up in a situation where you favour people because they are part of a certain community."
Audrey Hanard

Idealised meritocracy

Meritocracy...this topic has occupied my mind over the past few years. Meritocracy has been ingrained in me from a young age: if you want something, work for it, and you will succeed. Afterwards, I realised that I needed to work a bit harder than others to obtain the same results. Then, I saw people struggling and still not getting what they had hoped for. Somehow, I felt that this principle was more idealistic than realistic. Reality is more complex. A lot of people work very hard, and yet they don't succeed. Others don't work hard, and they do succeed. The notion that you get what you deserve is not always true. Dare I say *often* not true? Michael Sandel's essay, "The Tyranny of Merit", helped me put my thoughts into words. This well-known professor at Harvard University explains how meritocracy can actually do more harm than good. If you deserve what you have, then you have no responsibility to assist others. Indeed, if they do not have it, then it is because they did not work hard enough, right? In the system of aristocracy, people know they are born into privilege, so it is their duty to assist the poor. The meritocracy approach leads the individual to believe that he or she is not privileged, but rather deserving.

What about your skills, talents, network, character, health, self-confidence...? People seeing their professional life as a success should acknowledge all the support they got. We all got some help at some point. It can vary from that person who introduced you to a current colleague, that student who commented on your university thesis, the parents who loved you and raised you to have self-confidence, that spouse who stopped her or his career to focus on family while you were launching your business, that partner who financed your first activity, that mentor who boosted you when you stopped believing in yourself...We should never forget where we come from and all the people on our way who supported us in one way or another. Our privileges may be different, but most of them are there through luck, not merit.

———

> *The meritocracy approach leads the individual to believe that he or she is not privileged, but rather deserving.*

———

I remember a student at the university who worked so hard to achieve average results, and another who began reviewing her lessons one month before the exam and then succeeded with better grades. Or that other student who worked in order to cover her own basic expenses such as rent and food, dreaming of one day skiing with her friends during the holidays. Using those examples, one may conclude that there is meritocracy since both students received diplomas at the end. Yes, but at what cost? No social life, no extracurricular activities, so no network, hence difficulty finding a job. In spite of studying more or starting their careers earlier, they did not achieve their goals equally. Whether it is a lack of method, financial resources, competencies, education, guidance, or self-confidence, we are not on a level playing field. If equality does not exist, how can meritocracy work?

———

Entitlement endangers the notion of the common good and solidarity.

———

Entitlement endangers the notion of the common good and solidarity. Empathy becomes impossible. Human respect for less fortunate people tends to disappear. Should the more privileged students help them, by sharing notes and summaries, for example? Part of the work could be shared in order to alleviate the pain of the less privileged, without harming the gains of the more advantaged.

> **"** *The meritocratic conviction that people deserve whatever riches the market bestows on their talents makes solidarity an almost impossible project. Why do the successful owe anything to the less-advantaged members of society? The answer to this question depends on recognising that, for all our striving, we are not self-made and self-sufficient, finding ourselves in a society that prizes our talents is our good fortune, not our due.[54]* **"**
> **Michael J. Sandel**

Sandel proposes using a lottery for selecting candidates, with their qualifications as a pre-requisite: "The lottery of the qualified." It is his solution for removing the hubris generated by meritocracy and integrating the role of luck. He takes the case of admission to prestigious universities.

> **"** *Rather than engage in the exceedingly difficult and uncertain task of trying to predict who among them are the most surpassingly meritorious, choose the entering class by lottery. In other words, toss the folders of the qualified applicants down the stairs, pick up 2,000 of them, and leave it at that.[55]* **"**
> **Michael J. Sandel**

Along with bringing humility to the selection process, his proposal also removes unconscious bias. Personal preferences have no bearing on the choice. No matter how hard you try, you will still have a bias. Let's try this concept. Consider the situation in which you need to hire a designer. Firstly, the job opening should be published in a variety of networks and in a language that fits. The reach of your campaign is successful: 150 resumes are sent in.

The second step is to analyse the criteria. Imagine you are seeking someone with a graduate degree, five years' experience, trilingual, and familiar with Adobe tools. Following a simple check, you create two piles:
- Yes, the candidate answers the conditions
- No, the candidate does not answer the conditions.

There is no "perhaps", it is a matter of simple facts. The underlying assumption is that what is stated on the resume is accurate... A third step entails entering these variables into a tool (excel or whatever) and conducting a lottery. The candidate who was presented in a random way is hired. You may find this harsh. It is nonetheless necessary to have human contact, so you can adapt the process accordingly. For example, you select five individuals for an interview. There will be some potential bias when picking those candidates, as you will still need to have "the feeling". In spite of this, the five individuals selected may not have even been considered without this process. As a result, discrimination can be significantly reduced.
Perfect?
No.

If there are only women in the department, you would like to favour a man (yes, this is also possible). The "lottery of the qualified" will not allow for a preference (except for the five drawn). You can model the lottery to put, for instance, a factor two when the gender is male, versus one when the gender is female. A similar adaptation can be applied for any positive discrimination necessary in the workplace.
Perfect?
No.

The college degree was specified in your conditions. The whole population does not have the opportunity to go to university. Not because of their talents; many factors enter into balance: self-confidence, family perspectives, school stimulation...

Obviously, you need some specifications, but you should ask yourself: is this really necessary? If not, remove it, as you will indirectly discriminate against and miss talented people.

As a leader, you can initiate a snowball effect that will be beneficial to both your company and society at large.

This is just one solution. There is no perfect way. As a leader, you will not be able to resolve all social injustices. Nonetheless, you can act at your level and initiate a snowball effect that will be beneficial to both your company and society at large.

"We're not doing Diversity, Equity and Inclusion for charity. It impacts the bottom line."
Ilham Kadri

Culturally living

The OPEN model invites us to embrace profile inclusiveness. Indeed, diversity, equality, and inclusiveness are primarily determined by appearance in society rather than in the workplace. For instance, I am an owner, and you would like to rent my house. I'm racist, I don't like your face, I'll refuse you. Then there will be an impact on your life, on your socio-economic level and on the future of your children. In other words, it is like a vicious circle based only on appearances: without adequate housing, education, or employment, people can become trapped in a low socio-economic status. It goes through to the recruitment, where we still have this discrimination based on the appearance of the person, even if it is unconscious. Even though you can say "I don't like you" in society, once in the same company, you are forced to work with that person. Then you will get past your first judgment because you have little or no choice. In the beginning you may resist but in the end you will see more than the colour of his or her skin or what he or she is wearing, or his or her general sexual preference or whatever. Then it will come to something that I believe is even trickier in companies: the diversity of profiles. For instance, I will have more problems because I'm very direct and my colleague does not say what she thinks. How can I be included with my own personality? In a company, the conflict will occur more based on the people's profile than based on their appearance.

"The difference between society and a company is that it is easier to live in an isolated bubble in society than in a company. So, companies are places where concrete engagement with diversity and inclusion is inevitable. And that is a great thing.

It also highlights a very important evolution: companies are organisations within society that elicit more trust than many other institutions, particularly given the recent pandemic crisis. Companies are places where openness and transparency are often stronger than outside. Where values of diversity, inclusion and equity are promoted, at international and even global levels. Places with often more freedom than some of the societies in which they operate.

Without being naïve, I would say that companies are emerging as much more than organisations designed to create economic value in a Darwinian business environment; they are places where lives can be fully lived."
Pierre Gurdjian

There is no doubt that in some countries, companies are more open than society as a whole. Even in Belgium, observing the media and political debate, you may believe that the country has many issues related to diversity of culture, while in many private companies, there are no such issues. Within a company, departments can have their own culture, based on the profile of employees and type of job. Some functions are structurally seen as "enemy". I once despised a colleague in a role (and he despised me), then when he changed to another job, we collaborated well together. I then realised that the problem was not him; it was the embedded hate-relationship between the two departments. For instance, sales people think that marketing is out of touch with reality, developers are seen as robots, business analysts have no idea about IT, etc. A company needs to have a strong culture; this is what creates commitment, loyalty, pride, motivation of the staff. The same is true for a team: how often do we see team building where one team plays against another for fun? But with this strong culture comes a whole series of consequences. There is a thin line between being proud of your department and thinking you are the best – that others are less good. The country culture also intervenes in the company's culture.

"I don't believe that there is a one-size-fits-all approach. Culture can be a barrier to implementing Diversity, Equity, and Inclusion worldwide. We see, for example, that speaking up when we witness a non-inclusive behaviour is a bigger challenge in Asia than in other parts of the world, and requires more targeted actions. In the US, we are used to speaking up – less in Asia, less in Europe. You need to make your organisation aware of that."

Ilham Kadri

If we want to work on diversity and inclusiveness, we must not only think about appearance but about personality profiles, we must not only think internal / external to the company, but internal / external to the departments too. Since this culture is strong, we might as well work on it so that it is as open as possible. This way, you reach two goals with the same effort. Unfortunately, working on culture is not that obvious, as it is a long-term investment. Going back to the words of

Pierre Gurdjian, culture is an integrative concept that cannot be consciously built. Defining a common mission is a good start to align on a company / department culture. Mikaël Wornoo links diversity with the common goal and sees a difference depending upon the size of the group.

"A company is a group, where you have one thing in common: you work for the same company. In society at large, it's very hard to say. You need to have something in common to create the group. The larger group, the larger the diversity, the harder it is to be inclusive. It's very easy to be included in a group of two or three. It's very hard to be inclusive with ten million people. At some point, anyone is going to feel excluded."
Mikaël Wornoo

It is indeed more difficult to include millions of people, but the benefits are even greater. As the saying has it, "No pain, no gain", right? Thierry Geerts sees a difference in the leverage you have as a CEO. Audrey Hanard supports this point by pointing out that work is one of the society's communities that can have an impact.

"Society is a kind of big company, or a company is a little society. That is why in French 'société' is the name for both. The advantage of a company is that you probably can decide and correct faster. If a CEO takes that seriously, you can have an impact today. You will not change everything, but you can make sure that people from diverse origins are more included."
Thierry Geerts

"Society is a sum of communities. One of the communities is work, where diversity and inclusion can be built. If at work, you feel you are being accepted and your contributions are valued, also because of your diversity, you will probably have a different perspective on society. You will use those skills to reach out and be more inclusive outside of work as well. One supports the other. If you want to build citizens who feel good and want to do good for their communities, work is one very concrete space to start with."
Audrey Hanard

This mismatch can have an impact on the projects you manage. For instance, Isabel Verstraete worked for an Art Festival and shares her experience on how easily we can discuss issues we don't understand.

"We are talking about how we can invite the inhabitants of other neighbourhoods in Antwerp to a festival, though they never show up at this kind of event. But the people around the table are all white, all living on the 'right' side of Antwerp. What solutions can we find? We have no clue. We are biased, we are not in their shoes; we don't live there. We should have representatives of those communities around the table."
Isabel Verstraete

For DEI to live in your organisation, it must be embedded in your company culture. Based on my experiences in private companies, public and private foundations, non-profit organisations and public institutions, I did not see a pattern of more or less inclusiveness linked to a sector. Having a societal goal does not make the organisation more inclusive. Having a financial goal does not make the organisation less inclusive. The how is not necessarily linked to the why. Ibrahim Ouassari shares the observation, with a nuance with regards to the hierarchical level.

"This difference is linked to the culture of the company. A chain of garage owners can have gender parity if the company culture lends itself to it. I see less diversity in the private sector, but in some, there are possibilities to break the glass ceiling. While in the public sector, there may be more diversity but they are limited to lower hierarchical functions."
Ibrahim Ouassari

Another question that often pops up in DEI debate: do you want inclusion only for your consumers, (e.g., your sales) or also internally? One cannot go without the other. If your internal staff does not reflect the society, your marketing budget will not be well spent. Hanan Challouki usually sees a great level of good intentions at the top but questions the human aspect of marketing DEI.

"There's a big difference when it comes to awareness and action. Commercial institutions invest a lot of money in diversity and inclusion, but mostly for marketable reasons. But you still must consider those audiences in your internal processes. Do you only want me as a consumer, or would you also hire me if I was applying for a job?"
Hanan Challouki

The company culture is shaped by each and every one of us. The essence of who we are, what we were, and what we intend to become. A strong impact is certainly attributed to the founders. Like a marriage, the initial principles are considered standards. Any deviation will have to be discussed, agreed upon. If you are married to someone who does not work and takes care of the main household activities, the norm is to provide the money while the other takes care of the domestic duties. All the equilibrium will change if, after five years, your partner decides to work. However, you will still have it ingrained in your mind that you find delicious meals ready every evening. The rules of the game are established when you establish a new organisation. This does not mean the culture of the organisation is fixed: the first people who will join will shape it with you, and it will evolve with departures and arrivals, as each one brings their own contribution. Almost the same is true when it comes to creating a new department within a large organisation, although we would not have the stress of funding. Even if the corporate culture has an influence, each department, each branch unit has a culture of its own. In the same company, you can have very open and less open atmospheres. For instance, I had a bad experience when I returned from maternity leave in a team where all members were men around fifty years old, who thought that arriving at 9h30 was "taking the morning off" and leaving at 5pm was "taking the afternoon off". In the beginning, those comments stressed me. I was working a lot and without breaks just to catch up. My first kid was very difficult at night; some days I went to sleep at 6am to wake up at 7am. Imagine you arrive at work the quickest you can after dropping your five-month old baby at the nursery, and you still get negative remarks.

One day I had had enough and just told them, "You arrive at 8h30 but you spend almost an hour at the coffee machine chatting. You leave at 6h30 but you take more than one hour for lunch and several coffee breaks. I may arrive later, but I am fully productive, and l am not late with a single task. So, stop bothering me." I am not sure they understood my point but at least they did not say anything again (at least not in front of me). This team has a presenteeism view: the hours you spend in the office count as work. Obviously, I quickly changed teams to join a younger one, where nobody cared about the amount of time you were actually present. All that mattered was: do you deliver according to plan? Do you manage your work, or do you make your colleagues do it? And there was a real team spirit. A colleague had difficulties at the end of her pregnancy, and she even arrived around 11am some days. No complaints, no remarks, just encouragement. What I loved about that team is that men as well as women said, "No, I cannot. It is my day to get my kids from school." It makes it so easy if you can just say it without being timid about it. Hopefully, younger generations tend to more parity in the education of their children. This evolution is not only profitable for women's careers, but also men's rights.

Coming back from my second maternity leave was no better: it led to the end of my previous career. Obviously, this was not the only factor (my societal commitment became my priority), but it helped me feel more confident in my decision.

While I was on leave, there were reorganisations and a change in location. I was absent for almost a year due to a difficult pregnancy. During the first two months, I worked from my couch. However, homework was not as common at that time as it is today, and even though my previous company was ahead of the curve in this area, I was unable to continue. Additionally, my gynaecologist was rather upset to learn that I was still working. As it was sudden, I did not pack prior to my absence. I asked some colleagues to pack my belongings and hoped to find all of it when I returned.

On the day I returned, I was unsure of where to sit. While wandering around the large open space, I asked around: "Do you know where my team is?" Finally, when I arrived, no one from the team was expecting me. "Oh, you are back already? I thought it would be next week." "No, it was today. I even confirmed with the manager last week." The manager was travelling and apparently did not inform the team. As I sat down, I took a deep breath. I opened my computer and attempted to connect to the network. Obviously, nothing was functioning properly. While I was down inspecting the cables, someone arrived and said, "Hello, you're in my seat." He was a Parisian colleague who used to sit at my desk when he was in Brussels. My colleague responded, "No longer; she is back from her leave." To which he replied, "Hmph. Where should I go now?"

If I had not felt welcome before, this was the icing on the cake. But it was still not the end.

Afterwards, a colleague came by and said, "I was looking for you. How are you? Let's grab a coffee!" Finally, someone had remembered me. While walking through the floor, I noticed that my chair was being used by someone else. It was an ergonomic chair marked with a sticker. I asked the person to return it to me.
- No, it's mine, he answered.
- No, it's mine, I said.
- No, it's mine, he repeated.
- No, it's mine, I insisted (I could go on like this forever).
- Look, what is written on this sticker? Ihsane Haouach. That's her, said my colleague.

The guy took out a post-it note, wrote his name, put it on the chair and asked, "What is written on this sticker?" I was so overwhelmed! Aside from his rudeness, I did not blame him: he had used a comfortable chair for six months, then a stranger tried to take it away from him. Upon my colleague's explanation and patient negotiation, he finally decided to return it to me (by pushing the chair towards me). As I moved my chair to my supposed desk, I came across souvenirs that I had purchased in Mexico (small animals whose heads oscillate when you type) on another desk. I took them back without a word. At the coffee corner, a man was drinking from a cup with Gaudi mosaics that I had bought in Barcelona. I asked, "I am sorry, is that yours?" He answered, "No, I found it in an empty desk." At least, this one was honest. I asked him to kindly give it back to me when he finished, which he did, after washing it (not everybody was rude).

It is not the first or, unfortunately, the last time that someone has returned from leave feeling excluded. Ilham Kadri experienced similar circumstances.

—

"One of the most difficult times in my career was when I was on maternity leave. A new organisational chart had been made, and they didn't put my name on it. Some colleagues called me to ask: 'Are you not coming back?' I answered, 'Of course I'm coming back!' I took four months of maternity leave; I wanted to enjoy some time with my baby. I was a highly performing colleague, but the management told me: 'Don't worry, you can take it slow, you are not going to travel a lot.' They didn't ask me the question. Being back didn't feel good, so I left the company. My son was six months old, my husband had just resigned, so we left, and I found a new job in another country.

The maternity leave issue stayed with me. I had always hoped to do something about it. That's why one of the first measures I took at Solvay was to launch 16 weeks of co-parental leave, regardless of gender, orientation, or location. Last year, 200 babies enjoyed having their fathers at home. It is great, and I'm sure they help their spouses as well."

Ilham Kadri

—

Throughout my life, I have believed that society discriminates against women in their role as mothers. During my pregnancy, I experienced such pressure to be a superwoman, to perform as usual while carrying a life, because the alternative is to be seen as weak. After giving birth, it is not as easy to leave your baby when you are not ready, because "It's time to come back", "The holidays are over." However, when I had my first child and witnessed my husband returning to work after only ten days with a broken heart and asking me for our baby's picture every quarter of an hour, I realised that society discriminates against men regarding their paternity. It was a real mentality switch. Men have the right to spend quality time with their children, as well as the right to take decent paternity leave. (Nonetheless, I am not claiming that current maternity leave is decent.) There is more to it than just the economic value of women's work; there is also the social value of parents' love (which can undoubtedly be valued economically as well). Women and men can both benefit from feminism, as it promotes equality for both genders. The feminism movement must also be inclusive. Sexism is not confined to a gender.

———

Women and men can both benefit from feminism, as it promotes equality for both genders.

———

A colleague asked his human resources partner for one day of parental leave a week. She requested, "Why can't your wife take it?" He had to repeat the process twice to make it happen. Apparently, for that female employee, only women should take care of their kids.

We are not less committed employees because we take time off for our loved ones or for ourselves. As a matter of fact, we will be more engaged if the balance between work and life is right for us. This is the reason behind safe spaces creation. Ideally the whole work environment must be a safe space, but let's face it, it is almost impossible. So, you need to structure specific spaces for your employees to share and discuss their main struggles, where they can be themselves without judgment, which as a result will boost their self-confidence (and then their performance).

Audrey Hanard shares the best practices at Dalberg, where diversity and equity monthly calls were set up on a regular basis. Speakers are invited and members share their topics. Decisions are made as a team on actions to be implemented, to cultivate an open atmosphere.

Anonymous questionnaires can also help if you use the replies to act on. There is nothing worse than asking people for their opinion if nothing is done afterwards: it is better to not inquire about anything than give them false hope. Those surveys can also help you create ombud groups that focus on topics that might benefit your team members.

Safe spaces are needed not only for discussions, but also for working. In your office, are there sufficient quiet and collaborative areas for your employees to work according to their preferences? Depending on their profiles, their preferences will differ, but they will not be fixed. It will depend on their level of energy at the moment, the type of task performed, and the interactions they have with direct and indirect colleagues. As a leader, your role is not to determine when they will need which type of space, but to guarantee that they have access to enough rooms, so they are always comfortable. The workplace is like a second home: one needs to feel at ease.

Silence means silence

Early in my career, I realised that my profile is an influential one. It was not that obvious at school where I did not have the self-confidence to be myself. It became clearer at the university where I became aware of my capacity to influence others. At the beginning, I thought it was nice, empowering. It clearly flattered my ego to see conversations going the way I wanted. Then, I started change management projects, and my propensity to dominate became an obstacle. I left meetings thinking agreement had been reached when it had not. I missed valuable inputs from more introverted persons because I did not give them enough room to speak up. I started analysing myself and asked some colleagues to criticise me. In the process, it was important that the people assigned to that task were trustworthy: it is hard enough to receive feedback, so the person giving it must be credible and well meaning. The first observation was that I always spoke first in meetings. In that way, I was setting up a direction.

A second one was that even though I asked if everyone was okay, I interpreted silence as a yes. Silence is neither a yes, nor a no, neither is it a perhaps. Silence cannot be interpreted. I learned that any interpretation from the receptor must be validated by the emitter. I started applying two rules: first, never be the first one to speak up; second, ask for a clear answer and give time if nobody is ready. It was hard. Remember I told you that I speak fast, I want work to be done rapidly and I am quickly bored. There I was, waiting patiently for others to actively participate. The result was incredible. I heard things I would never have thought about. Of course, if everyone follows the rule "Never be the first to speak up," nobody will say a word. But this rule is adapted for the dominant extroverts, who speak before or while thinking. The goal is not to keep them quiet; their ideas should also be heard. Anyhow, asking them to remain silent would be torture; they would always speak out... It is simply a matter of regulating their extrovert abilities. Introverts need to moderate their habit to think twice. By recognising and adjusting your natural self, you will be able to interact more easily with others. A leader should be able to organise meetings in an open way, to ensure active participation of all profiles.

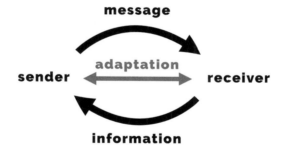

___

To let the others be natural, I had to open my natural self to learn patience. That empathy enabled me to find a common safe space with my co-workers.

___

To let the others be natural, I had to open my natural self to learn patience. That empathy enabled me to find a common safe space with my co-workers.

> **"** *Be yourself; everyone else*
> *is already taken.* **"**   **Oscar Wilde**

You just need a quarter

Accepting the natural self of someone else consists also of accepting disagreement. That is the tension between openness and naturalness. Not everyone will find your initiatives interesting; some may fight against them while others may be indifferent. In fact, you don't even need to have everyone on board: you just need 25% of them. In their study, Damon Centola, Joshua Becker, Devon Brackbill, and Andrea Baronchelli demonstrate the existence of a tipping point of 25% in the dynamics of changing social conventions (although this value is not universal in all social systems). After driving them to choose a name for their group, confederates were sent to change the established name. Once they reached a committed minority of a least 25% of the population, they consistently succeeded at convincing the group to adopt another name. Sometimes, just one extra person could trigger this tipping point. Will you be this person?

Predicted tipping points in social stability[56]

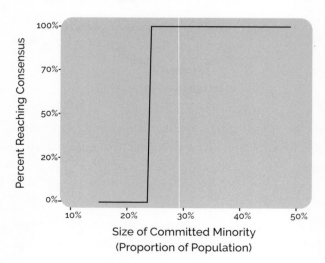

Conclusion

René Magritte understood the essence of the OPEN way before I was even born. The surrealist painter played with our perception of reality and the mental representations that we make of it. "This is not a pipe" written above a painting of a pipe illustrates the limits of appearances. The use of an apple to conceal a face is an effective method of highlighting characteristics that are not readily apparent.

The human mind is naturally curious about the unknown. The more we are unable to view an individual's face, the more determined we will be to search for it. As soon as our eyes are drawn to it, they cease to search. However, we have not yet encountered the person. Physical appearance is not indicative of a person's character.

" *Everything we see hides another thing; we always want to see what is hidden by what we see.* **"** **René François Ghislain Magritte**

Upon viewing this piece of art, I am transported to a foggy sky.

There are times when I feel the need to go to the sea, as the horizon seems endless there. The deep blue (or grey, as in the Belgian sea) helps my mind evade. The air from the sea helps us to breathe slowly, to hear, and to heal our bodies and minds. Despite the low and often gloomy sky, light is still present, as the sun is always somewhere.

Masking our profile prevents us from being ourselves while on the contrary, it helps us to stay ourselves. Blocking parts of our profile limits our potential. Were we to reveal everything, would we be liked as we are? Cutting fragments of our personality helps to keep it safe. Were we to reveal everything, would we remain as we are?

Promoting diversity, equity, inclusion, and inclusiveness begins with feeling the intention. The goal is to engage because it is the right thing to do, not because it is fashionable (of course, that is convenient). The objective must be clearly stated, regardless of whether it is to strive for a more inclusive society or to improve business performance. Openness allows us to agree to disagree and disagree to agree. Neither we nor our colleagues are immune to making mistakes. Nobody is perfect. It is still difficult for me to accept any deficiencies, especially my own. Rather than hiring individuals who are similar to us as a means of making us feel comfortable, we should look for people who complement us. Managing a team requires consideration of differences in needs, thus fair and justified exceptions are necessary to achieve equity beyond equality.

There is something about the calm and steadiness of the man depicted in the painting that I admire. It appears as if he takes time for contemplating profound thoughts. Making a right decision requires patient consideration of our options. Depending on the context, the collective decision process varies. It should not be rushed to satisfy an immediate need while ignoring long term impacts.
For any change to last, continual learning and development should be encouraged among employees. Positive reinforcement is preferable to sanctioning incorrect behaviour, regardless of how it was taught to us.

As with the hands in the painting, there are parts of us that are in the shadows and there are parts of us that are in the spotlight. We need a bit of shadow to shine. Our actions are influenced by our experiences, our fears, our ambitions, our character, and our role in the world. As we adapt to all of these factors, our behaviour changes. From last year to this year, I have not just added a candle to my birthday cake, but everything that has happened has had an impact on me. In Arabic, there is an adage, "kol haja fiha kheir" كل حاجة فيها خير, which can be translated as, "In each thing, there is a blessing". Hopefully, we will be able to make positive use of our experiences, even those that are painful.

Considering that empathy levels are often triggered by personal events, active listening is essential in order to facilitate collaboration. We rely on our intuition to support rational decisions. Sometimes we want a seat at the table, and sometimes we prefer to leave (quietly or not). In addition to hiding parts of our personalities, the apple helps us disguise our emotions. Even without facial expressions, our bodies communicate for us. When I observe the posture of the Son of Man with straight shoulders, I perceive it to be tense. His tie is so tangled that I would love to loosen it a bit, as a way of opening his mind and encouraging him to be natural.

Being natural while remaining open is a challenge. Tension between the two will vary, depending on the context and the culture. A safe space must be found in which everyone can be himself or herself, without impinging on the space of the others. What is the limit? The choices are personal. What is true for one person may not be true for another. We are inclined to believe that every decision made at work is a business decision: this is not true. First and foremost, everything is personal. No matter how rational the choice may be, it will always be a personal one. With the mix of all our individual values, culture is constantly evolving. Culture must be lived in order to exist, whether it is a societal or corporate culture. Forcing the inclusion of missing representations can be a practical short-term solution, supported by sustainable actions for cultural change.

With this book, my intent is to provide another perspective on a key theme. With many years of experience in private, public, and societal organisations, I felt it was the right time to pause, reflect, and share. The content was designed to be pragmatic and philosophical – a quick wins result from long-term vision. I hope that the stories narrated by the interviewees and me will provide inspiration for any leader trying to improve daily operations in a lasting manner.

The OPEN way is a framework to engage structural change in your organisation, enabling your people to develop:

- Openness, the quality of being receptive to different ideas, opinions, or arguments, regardless of the source.
- Patience, the quality to accept and endure changes, desired or not, with quietness.
- Empathy, the ability to sense other people's emotions and connect to their thoughts, experiences, and feelings.
- Natural, the inherent sense of one's personality, expressed through effortless endeavours.

Depending on the level of maturity and commitment, different approaches are possible. The first item on your list is to decide whether you want to take your organisation a step further or not.

Your intention determines your objectives.

Your actions determine the success of those objectives.

Even though it is natural to be drawn to the improved profitability argument, it is important not to forget that DEI is a matter of basic humanity at its heart.

There will be obstacles, but with willingness, everything can be overcome.

A quarter of committed individuals is all it takes to make a difference... The question is: do you want to be part of it?

Thanks

Thanking is a challenging exercise because I am always worried that I will forget someone. In order to cover all the bases, I would like to say thank you to all of you (even you, as reader), for surrounding me with friendship, benevolence, respect, or simply consideration.

First and foremost, I would like to thank God, who blessed me with the intelligence to think, the skills to write, the resilience to continue, the love of my family, the support of my friends and the inspiration of new encounters.

My parents were my first supporters: they believed in me from the moment I was born, which is not really objective. Nevertheless, their confidence in me grew with my achievements, which encouraged me to reach ever higher heights and create a positive cycle of success.

My husband's devotion is an enabler for my projects. His brilliance has helped me navigate turbulent waters. Whenever a storm sweeps me away, he is swept away even more. My partner's unconditional support for my choices and for the engaged woman that I am is my anchor.

While my children do not understand everything yet, their existence helps me to see things from a different perspective. They bring joy and happiness into our home with their laughter; their cries make silence worthwhile. A friend once asked me, "Do you sleep at night with all that is happening in your life?" To which I replied, "With a baby, I do not have the luxury of having insomnia. So yes, I sleep (when I am able to)."

I had the honour of being born after incredible siblings who loved me and forgave my many attempts to pull their hair out or pour my meal on them. Whatever we do, our confidence in each other remains unwavering. My (step-)sisters, my (step-)brothers and my (step-)parents are what makes our families a model of diversity. All of us live different lives, yet we are united by the bond of love.

This book would not have been possible without the twelve people who trusted me with their stories. Some of my interviews were made possible through Belgium's 40 under 40 program, for which I am extremely grateful. The alchemy of different thoughts demonstrates the beauty of diversity. Thanks to Audrey Hanard, Ilham Kadri, Ibrahim Ouassari, Isabel Verstraete, Isabelle Ferreras, Francis Blake, Hanan Challouki, Mikaël Wornoo, Pierre Gurdjian, Thibaut Georgin, Thierry Geerts, Satish Kumar for partnering their voices with mine.

In our lives, we meet many people. Several are valuable, some are disposable, some are irreplaceable. Alexandre Pycke and Harold Boël are among those irreplaceable friends who, with Francis Blake, enriched the book with their challenges.

My sincere gratitude extends to my editors at LannooCampus, for their kindness and confidence. Our collaboration has been enjoyable from the first contact, and I felt certain that my book would flourish in their hands. Their valuable feedback and insights are what elevated this manuscript to a higher level.

Furthermore, I wish to thank all the people I met during my various experiences: at university, at work, and throughout all social activities. Consciously or unconsciously, all the events, discussions, and debates I have had over the past few years have been used to construct the OPEN way.

Endnotes

1   "Catch the Sun" is the second single from Doves' debut studio album Lost Souls, released on 29 May 2000.
2   "Fruit étrange(r)", Ras El Hanout asbl, 2010
3   Sophocles, & Heaney, S. (2004). The Burial at Thebes : Sophocles' Antigone.
4   United Nations, Gender Ratio in the World in 2021, https://population.un.org/wpp/Download/Standard/Population/
5   Eurostat, Population on 1 January by age and sex. (s. d.). [Base de données ; 2022 https://ec.europa.eu/eurostat/databrowser/
    view/ DEMO_PJAN__custom_4561662/default/table ? lang=en].
6   Smillie, L. (2017, août 15). Openness to Experience : The Gates of the Mind. Scientific American. https://www.scientificameri-
    can.com/article/openness-to-experience-the-gates-of-the-mind/
7   Neuro-linguistic programming (NLP) is a psychological approach to communication, personal development, change man-
    agement and psychotherapy, created by Richard Bandler and John Grinder in 1975.
8   Untapping the True Potential of Belgian Workforce Diversity. (2022b, décembre 1). BCG Global x Google. https://www.bcg.
    com/publications/2022/belgium-untapping-the-true-potential-of-belgian-workforce-diversity
9   Holiday, R. (2016b). Ego is the Enemy : The Fight to Master Our Greatest Opponent. Profile Books.
10 Holiday, R. (2016b). Ego is the Enemy : The Fight to Master Our Greatest Opponent. Profile Books.
11 Written in the Universal Declaration of Human Rights, Article 29, and detailed in national laws.
12 American psychologist Harry Harlow was interested to study an uneasy topic : love. With the help from his wife, Margaret
    Kuenne, he created the Monkey Mother Experiment in the 1960s. He removed young rhesus from their natural mothers af-
    ter birth, and provided those babies with a choice between different « mothers » : one made of wire but giving food, another
    made of soft terrycloth but giving no food. The infant monkeys visited the wire mother for food and spent their time with
    the soft terrycloth. Harlow concluded that affection was the primary force behind the need for closeness. Later, he went fur-
    ther and isolated baby monkeys for up to twenty-four hours to see the impacts. The monkeys went out intensely distrubed.
    Although famous, this experiment is judged as terrible unethical and cruel with regards to the monkeys.
    Cherry, K. (2023). Harry Harlow and the Nature of Affection. Verywell Mind. https://www.verywellmind.com/harry-harlow-
    and-the-nature-of-love-2795255
13 A consequence of the Socialist Republic of Romania's pro-natality policy under Nicolae Ceaușescu, inciting families to give
    birth and abandon their child to the state for a "better" education.
14 Hughes, V. (2020). Romanian orphans – a human tragedy, a scientific opportunity | Aeon Essays. Aeon. https://aeon.co/
    essays/romanian-orphans-a-human-tragedy-a-scientific-opportunity
15 Daniel Kahneman is a senior scholar at Eugene Higgins, professor of psychology emeritus at Princeton University and a
    professor of public affairs at the Woodrow Wilson School of Public and International Affairs. He received the 2002 Nobel
    Prize in Economic Sciences for his pioneering work with Amos Tversky on decision-making.
16 Kahneman & Tversky, 1973; Kahneman, Slovic & Tversky, 1982; Tversky & Kahneman, 1974
17 Kahneman & Tversky, 1979
18 Kahneman, D. (2011). Thinking, Fast and Slow. Penguin UK. Page 71.
19 #BlackLivesMatter was founded in 2013 in response to the acquittal of Trayvon Martin's murderer and gained further
    international attention following the death of George Floyd in 2020. It is a decentralised political and social movement
    highlighting racism, discrimination, and racial inequality experienced by black people.
20 FORTUNE is a global media organisation dedicated to helping its readers, viewers, and attendees succeed in business
    through storytelling.
21 Refinitiv is one of the world's largest providers of financial market data and infrastructure, serving over 40,000 institutions
    in approximately 190 countries.
22 Refinitiv. (s. d.). FORTUNE and Refinitiv encourage unprecedented corporate diversity disclosure and accountability through
    new measure up partnership. https://www.refinitiv.com/en/media-center/press-releases/2020/october/fortune-and-refini-
    tiv-encourage-unprecedented-corporate-diversity-disclosure-and-accountability-through-measure-up-partnership
23 Refinitiv. (s. d.-a). Diversity and Inclusion in the Workplace Report. https://www.refinitiv.com/en/resources/special-report/
    diversity-and-inclusion-at-workplace
24 Philippe Urfalino. The Rule of Non-Opposition. Opening Up Decision-Making by Consensus. Journal of Political Philosophy,
    2014. hal-01226344
    Philippe Urfalino is a sociologist, an author, director of research at C.N.R.S., and director of studies at EHESS Centre d'Etudes
    Sociologiques et Politiques Raymond Aron.

25 Bicameralism (opposed to unicameralism) consists of a legislature divided into two separate assemblies, chambers, or houses. According to the report "IPU PARLINE database: Structure of parliaments". ipu.org. 2022, 42% of world's national legislatures are bicameral 2022, and 58% are unicameral.

26 Mondragon corporate presentation, 2022 – https://www.mondragon-corporation.com/wp-content/uploads/docs/MDGN-pres-CORPORATIVA_EN.pdf

27 In the 1940s, psychologists Kenneth and Mamie Clark conducted experiments known as "the doll tests" to study the psychological effects of segregation on African-American children. Their subjects were aged between three to seven. The conclusion was that "prejudice, discrimination, and segregation" created a feeling of inferiority that damaged the self-esteem of African-American children.

28 For example, Toni Sturdivant in 2021 varied the conditions of the study, yet concluded that the black doll is systematically not chosen to play with, and if selected, mistreated.

29 Kimberlé Williams Crenshaw is an American civil rights advocate and a leading scholar of critical race theory. She is the co-founder of the African American Policy Forum and is a professor at the UCLA School of Law in Los Angeles and Columbia Law School in New York City, where she specialises in race and gender issues.

30 Crenshaw, Kimberlé Williams (1989) "Demarginalizing the Intersection of Race and Sex: A Black Feminist Critique of Antidiscrimination Doctrine, Feminist Theory and Antiracist Politics." University of Chicago Legal Forum 1989:139–67, p. 149

31 According to the World Migration Report 2015, after Dubai, Brussels is the city with the highest percentage of residents born abroad. More than six in ten Brussels residents were not born in Belgium. In 2023, Brussels is the fourth most diverse city with 31.7% residents born abroad.

32 Organizational Change Management | HR Insights | Gartner.com. (s. d.). Gartner. https://www.gartner.com/en/human-resources/insights/organizational-change-management

33 Types of Organizational Change & How to Manage Them | HBS Online. (2020, 20 mars). Business Insights Blog. https://online.hbs.edu/blog/post/types-of-organizational-change

34 Verna Myers is a world-known inclusion strategist, cultural innovator, social commentator, and Netflix's VP, Inclusion Strategy. White Men Roles | Vernã Myers. (2021, 16 septembre). [Vidéo]. Vernã Myers. https://www.vernamyers.com/online-training/white-men-roles/

35 Fatima Zibouh is responsible for the anti-discrimination department within the Brussels employment agency and is an expert on inclusion, discrimination, and diversity issues. TEDx Talks. (2022, 9 septembre). Pour une inclusion radicale ! | Fatima Zibouh | TEDxBrussels [Vidéo]. YouTube. https://www.youtube.com/watch?v=6wE3WZXT960

36 Helliwell, J. F. (2022, 18 mars). World Happiness Report 2022. The World Happiness Report. https://worldhappiness.report/ed/2022/

37 Diversity wins : How inclusion matters. (2020, 19 mai). McKinsey & Company. https://www.mckinsey.com/featured-insights/diversity-and-inclusion/diversity-wins-how-inclusion-matters

38 "The Mute Girl of Portici", an opera in five acts by Daniel Auber, with a libretto by Germain Delavigne, revised by Eugène Scribe, is known for its alleged role in the Belgian Revolution of 1830. The opera was chosen for a performance at the Théâtre de la Monnaie in Brussels on 25 August 1830, as part of King William I's festival in celebration of the 15th year of his reign. Although the day was already chosen by the rebels "Monday, the 23rd, fireworks; Tuesday, the 24th, illuminations; Wednesday, the 25th, revolution," people became more enthusiastic and daring with the opera songs "Amour sacre de la patrie" and "Aux armes". A crowd left the theatre and joined the demonstration for the revolution.

39 The mission of the Côte-à-Côte non-profit organisation is to create an environment that allows people affected by cerebral palsy to realise their life project through autonomy and solidarity to become active members of society. This project also allows the inhabitants and friends of Côte-à-Côte, whether they have disabilities, to be enriched by sharing a life experience.

40 The mission of the Demoucelle Parkinson Charity is to "provide funding to the world's most promising research projects and raise awareness about the impact of this fast-growing neurodegenerative condition." Patrick's story - Demoucelle Parkinson Charity. (2020, 16 novembre). Demoucelle. https://www.demoucelle.com/charity/%20about-parkinson/story/

41 Jacques Georgin was a teacher and member of the political party Front Démocratique des Francophones (FDF). In his honour, a street was named after him, a memorial was built, and the "Jacques Georgin Study Centre" was created.

42 Kenza Isnasni's parents were murdered in 2002 by a far-right extremist neighbour. Now she has created a foundation in their honour "Habiba Ahmed Foundation (HAF)".

43 This quote « The end justifies the means » is attributed to Niccolò Machiavelli, in his political treatise « The Prince » distributed in 1513, althought the phrase was not used in this wording and he brings a lot of nuance.

44 The Hermann Ebbinghaus' Forgetting Curve, published in 1885 and still widely used, demonstrates how information is lost over time when there is no attempt to retain it. Ebbinghaus, H. (1987). Memory : a contribution to experimental psychology. Annals of Neurosciences. https://doi.org/10.5214/ans.0972.7531.200408

45 As Edgar Dale's Cone of Experience in 1946, highlighting the interrelations of diverse types of medias and their individual positions in the learning process. He demonstrated that learners retain more information by what they "do" as opposed to what is "heard", "read" or "observed". Dale, Edgar. Audio-Visual Methods in Teaching, 3rd ed., Holt, Rinehart & Winston, New York, 1969, p. 108

46 Score in the CARE scan Isabel Verstraete developed. Verstraete, I. (2021). Does Your Brand Care ? : Building a Better World with the C A R E principles. Lannoo Meulenhoff - Belgium.

47 Many studies were realised over the year on the subject, like the one of Nielsen showing that consumers want a more personal connection in the way they gather information: Nielsen. (2022, 19 décembre). Getting closer : Influencers help brands build more personal consumer connections | Nielsen. Nielsen. https://www.nielsen.com/insights/2022/getting-closer-influencers-help-brands-build-more-personal-consumer-connections/

48 Kay Formanek is advisor, author, coach and speaker on the transformational power of diversity to organisations and society.

49 Formanek, K. (2021). Beyond D&I : Leading Diversity with Purpose and Inclusiveness. Palgrave Macmillan. Page 241.

50 Catalyst is a global non-profit supported by many of the world's most powerful CEOs and leading companies to help build workplaces that work for women. . Catalyst. (2022, août 30). Measuring for Change | Catalyst. https://www.catalyst.org/measuring-for-change/

51 Isabel Verstraete developed the CARE principles: a generic insight about taking care of people and the planet, as we live in turbulent times and companies simply must take better care of people and the planet. But there's more to it, CARE also stands for four shifts in our attitude that can change to become more future proof. CARE stands for: collaboration, agility, reliability, empathy. Diversity is part of agility in her model.

52 Kumar, S. (2021). Pilgrimage for Peace : The Long Walk from India to Washington. Green Books. Page 32.

53 The Friday Group is a group of young people aiming to bring innovative and realistic ideas to society. Vrijdaggroep — Inspiring policy through diversity. (2022, 4 septembre). Vrijdaggroep. https://www.v-g-v.be/

54 Sandel, M. J. (2020). The Tyranny of Merit : What's Become of the Common Good ? Penguin UK. Page 227.

55 Sandel, M. J. (2020). The Tyranny of Merit : What's Become of the Common Good ? Penguin UK. Page 185

56 Theoretical modeling of the proportion of outcomes in which the alternative behavior is adopted by 100% of the population. In this system, the number of agents (N) = 1000, the number of interactions (T) = 1000, the number of past interactions used in agent decisions (M) = 12. Centola, D., Becker, J. A., Brackbill, D., & Baronchelli, A. (2018). Experimental evidence for tipping points in social convention. Science, 360(6393), 1116-1119. https://doi.org/10.1126/science.aas8827.